MUTUAL RESPECT

Therapeutic Approaches To Working with People who have Learning Difficulties

Edited by David Brandon

Good Impressions Publishing Ltd.,
Hexagon House, Surbiton Hill Road,
Surbiton, Surrey KT6 4TZ.

(i)

First published in 1989 by Good Impressions Publishing Ltd
Hexagon House, Surbiton Hill Road, Surbiton, Surrey KT6 4TZ.

© 1989 Good Impressions Publishing Ltd

ISBN 1 871172 02 0

Front cover design: Marius Dean, London SW9. 01-627 4344

Printed by: Personal Print, London SW4. 01-498 0245

Typeset by: Typestream Graphics Ltd., London SW4. 01-498 0450

Dedicated to

Beverley Michael
of Cornerstone, Aberdeen,

whose questions about counselling
inspired this book.

CONTENTS

About the authors

David Barron spent over 20 years in an institution. His account of his experiences, privately published in four volumes, is the most revealing and vivid record we have of what it was like on the receiving end of 'services'. In describing his life story in such detail he has given us invaluable insight with which to approach the emotional problems of people with learning difficulties.

Nigel Beail is Principal Clinical Psychologist and Head of Specialty (People with Learning Difficulties) at the Keresforth Centre, Barnsley, and Lecturer in Clinical Psychology at the University of Sheffield. After obtaining a BA in psychology at Middlesex Polytechnic, he investigated father involvement in pregnancy, birth and early parenthood at the Thomas Coram Research Unit, University of London for which he was awarded a PhD in 1983. He then trained as a clinical psychologist at the University of Leeds.

Dr Beail has published numerous papers on fatherhood, physical disability, the quality of care provided for children with learning difficulties, assessment, psychotherapy and personal construct theory.

Margaret Heal was born in Canada. She holds a Bachelor of Arts and a Bachelor of Music degree from Queen's University (Canada) and Postgraduate Licentiate Diploma in Music Therapy from the Guildhall School of Music and Drama (London). She is currently Music Therapist at Leytonstone House, London, for adults with learning difficulties.

Ms Heal is a student supervisor on the Guildhall music therapy course and is studying part-time on the Observational Studies Course at the Tavistock Institute, London.

Pat Frankish is Senior Clinical Psychologist at St Mary's Hospital, Scarborough. She holds a BA from Hull University and trained in clinical psychology at Liverpool University, gaining a Master's degree in 1985. She also has a diploma for teaching children with severe learning difficulties.

Ms Frankish is presently involved in the development of services for people with learning difficulties in Scarborough.

Alison Buckley holds a BA(Hons) and a Diploma in Art Therapy, RATh, from Hertfordshire College of Art and Design. She is a Senior Art Therapist working in an institution for the care of people with learning difficulties.

Ms Buckley originally trained and practised as a graphic designer before becoming an art therapist. She is currently involved in Observation Studies at the Tavistock Institute, London.

Introduction

David Brandon

This book is intended as an introductory primer to help people who want to counsel people with learning difficulties deepen their knowledge. It is not meant to be comprehensive but it should be easy to read. Everything necessary should be explained. Just bring your ordinary human qualities. Ten years ago the overall question was, is such counselling possible? Now the question has changed to, how can we do it? We hope that Mutual Respect will be followed by many other similar books and papers on this subject.

Non-behaviourist introductory material on counselling people with learning difficulties is hard to find. There are no behaviourist approaches described here except that the last chapter, Professional Behaviours, provides some description of how it might be stood on its head. Behaviourist therapies are well documented in the field of learning difficulties - masses of research papers and tons of heavy tomes are devoted to it. Nothing sinister should be read into their omission. The writers who have contributed to this book are mainly influenced by psychodynamic theories and not necessarily antagonistic to behaviourist approaches. They describe alternative approaches which widen the options for therapeutic work in this field, so long dominated by behaviourism. They are more inclined to humanistic approaches than to the technical end of the continuum. However, there are many other options not described in this book - transactional analysis, cognitive therapy, gestalt therapy to name just a few - but there is a need for many other books, pamphlets and, most of all, videos. This small book can only meet a tiny part of that extensive need.

Our five writers are people from very different backgrounds who have mostly not met one another. Four of them would describe themselves as therapists, the fifth is a man with learning difficulties. All have extensive experience of the services and its many ways of damaging users and staff. Their work could be described as an attempt at repairing some of that damage.

In The Power to Heal? I describe the necessary expansion of different kinds of humanising processes - befriending, advocacy, individualised programme planning, various sorts of staff training - and ambitiously try to put the development of counselling and psychotherapy in the whole context of those. Some key dangers inherent in professionalising ordinary human qualities are identified. We must be careful not to blindly stumble into different and yet more sophisticated ways of colonising disabled people.

For the succeeding chapters, the writers were asked to keep to a common format. They describe the nature and theoretical basis of their work and illustrate it with two practical examples. In the exchange between therapists and subjects, the reader can see how the theories work in practice. Two of the writers are traditional psychodynamic therapists, although their professional contribution is much wider, merging into the academic world. The other two, although inspired by the same tradition, are using art and music as mediums. What all have written has both excited and instructed me. They are trying to honestly unite some theory and practice at an early stage in our understanding of the pain and suffering of disabled people. Their forms present some real conflicts for the ways in which the services currently operate. Both forms and services will have to undergo major changes.

As for myself, a Buddhist monk/psychotherapist, my approach is more eclectic. Humming Quietly is about teaching meditation in an adult training centre, a real conflict of traditions. Can people with learning difficulties gain anything from an essentially oriental practice? I feel the answer is a hopeful one.

David Barron is one of the most remarkable people I have met. He has contributed a chapter about his horrific experiences in various mental handicap services - from mental handicap hospital to hostel to adult training centre - and about how he survived. Now nearing pensionable age, he has spent a great deal of his adult life searching out his own history and has produced four fascinating and extensive volumes. His chapter is based on his life story and the nature of the pain and healing in his search.

The final chapter contains some visions for the future. It warns against the gimmick trap and expresses hope that we will become less coercive and intrusive and more gentle. It outlines the specific techniques of Gentle

Teaching developed at the University of Nebraska in the United States.

There is no attempt to tie the chapters together in an all-embracing overview of the subject. That is partly because I am not capable of such a feat but also because each chapter stands on its own as an example of practical pilgrimage. My main wish is that you will enjoy reading this book and find within it enrichment for your own practice.

A final introductory comment. An extremely respected friend responded to my enthusing about this book by saying, in his born-again normalisation tone, 'Sounds devaluing to me.' That completely dampened my enthusiasm. He explained that terms like counselling and psychotherapy imply that there is something medically wrong with the persons receiving it. We live in sad times if that is the case.

The Greek root of the term 'psychotherapy' is 'soul healing'. We all need help from time to time in bringing ourselves into something even roughly approximating to a harmonious whole. We undergo stresses and hardships as part of our ordinary human existence and seek solace and understanding. Some find it in close friendship; others in mountain walking; listening to music from Bach to Bob Dylan to UB 40; writing; romantic love; poetry; meditation; prayer; political action. My small sailing boat - a spiritual dream in glass fibre! - is of supreme importance to me.

However, some need the special kind of relationship that good counselling and psychotherapy can offer. We have been damaged often by the systems, our families, overwhelming traumas. As a boy I was constantly battered by my father. In my late twenties I sought help urgently when deep depression overtook me. I was close to suicide. The considerable psychotherapeutic help I received, along with great and constant love from my family, kept me going. Far from feeling devalued by it, psychotherapy helped me to re-evaluate my life and to grow stronger. That help should be readily accessible to people with learning difficulties who need it, in the same way as it has been to many others. Historically, it has not been. It would be tragic if this book contributed to a special breed of therapist who worked exclusively with 'special needs cases'. It would be wonderful if a whole generation of counsellors became less fearful and more able to assist those people with learning difficulties who feel in need of their help.

Even the ripest and rosiest of apples can have worms. Care in eating is to be recommended. Counselling is not without problems, especially if it is done badly and with little 'mutual respect'. Hopefully, the genuine enthusiasm of the writers of this book is tempered with sufficient agnosticism.

David Brandon

Chapter 1

The Power to Heal?

David Brandon

We have all been shaped by the relative richness or poverty of our emotional lives. We have learned to experiment, taking opportunities which bring joy or sadness. As children, we develop and mature largely through our relationships with peers and adults. As adults, we strive to develop a range of valued relationships reflecting and supporting our sense of self. We can usually avoid relationships in which we feel devalued and disliked.

Most of us operate in a wide variety of different settings without overwhelming anxiety. We may be more comfortable with certain kinds of people or locations than others but we can still function adequately on the margins of our ability. We pass through many different experiences: going to restaurants, theatres, cinemas; travelling in trains and cars; meeting people, from porters to bus conductors, councillors to car park attendants. Mainly we mix with non-devalued people. Few friends, the people we go to football matches with, share a house with, regularly accompany to restaurants, are in wheelchairs - fewer still have learning difficulties.

People often get their information about people with learning difficulties from negative and casual images. 'I thought of a Mongol girl who used to hang around our village. She was always dressed in ill-fitting clothes. The thought of this girl began to haunt me when I knew that Jennifer was a Down's baby. It took me months to realise that at least there was no reason why I couldn't buy Jennifer clothes that fit her perfectly.' (Hollins and Grimer, 1988). People with learning difficulties can grow up experiencing overwhelmingly low expectations from relatively powerful others. They are different in an essentially negative sense. They have been perceived as social deviants and consequently heavily stigmatised. Even those who love them, their parents, brothers and sisters, are immersed in a negative culture, a 'can't do culture'. Historically, the terms used to describe them - 'defectives' 'subnormals' 'mongols' - express fear and rejection of their humanity. Although like any cross-section of people they vary enormously from one another, they are often perceived as similiar; for example, it is said that 'all Down's syndrome people are bright and cheerful'. Often they have felt a burden to others, a problem to various professionals and used services which devalued them. *'I always felt I was a big bag of stones to my Mum and Dad as well as to my brother.'* (Brandon and Ridley, 1985).

Some sources are unexpected. Several years ago, Mencap produced an intensely devaluing poster which read 'WHEN MATTHEW'S 18 HE'S GOING TO UNIVERSITY....WHEN KEVAN'S 18 HE'S GOING NOWHERE....' These two boys were photographed side by side. Kevan obviously had learning difficulties. Elsewhere in this book, David Barron writes about his personal experience of stigma and exploitation.

The services have often not only failed to liberate these people but added to their disability. Ivan Illich (1975) calls this 'iatrogenic disorder', meaning that damage paradoxically comes from our attempts to help and heal. People have largely mixed with other severely disabled people, and been segregated from ordinary services like libraries, schools, colleges and workplaces. Friendships tend to be either with other devalued people or with paid staff. Segregated services are usually paternalistic and over-protective, sometimes even destructive and neglectful. They hinder the availability of necessary opportunities which enable personal development and emotional growth. Frequently, disabled people live their lives in a Wendy House world - a world coy about real wages and real sex. Mannoni points out that many mentally handicapped children are treated, and therefore behave, as objects. 'They are lived by other people, especially their mothers.' (Anderson, 1982).

The usual experience of handicapped people has been to attend special schools, put away from most of us. When they leave home, they live in hostels or long stay hospitals, not in ordinary houses and flats; they rarely gain worthwhile paid employment but attend adult training centres and receive 'therapy money', usually only £4 a week. Many feel thoroughly devalued as people. Nellie, a friend who attends an ATC, expressed that eloquently: 'We are not proper people. Neighbours treat us badly. The youths throw stones through our windows and put rubbish in our letter box.' (Personal communication).

Pauline, aged 26, lives near Warrington. 'When I was about 14 I went to Greenlane School. It was a slow school for slow people who can't read properly. All we could do was read, write and do sums in the morning, and in the afternoon you could do what you wanted - play music, paint or anything like that. It was no good for me. I wanted to do more.' (Brandon and Ridley, 1985). Pauline lives in a hostel and attends an ATC like many thousands of other handicapped people. She has been encouraged to think she is a 'low achiever' so she often feels 'not worthwhile'.

These comments by Pauline and Nellie illustrate how negative experiences affect people's self images. This stunts their personal confidence and the way they relate to the world. Our services create vicious circles which generate poor self images frustrating healthy individual growth and development.

If Pauline, Nellie and many others are to develop fully they need different and much improved services. We now understand a great deal about how to make those changes and considerably improve people's quality of life. We need a foundation of what Wolfensberger calls 'realistic optimism' which must include increasing opportunities for choices, involvement in decision-making processes and integration; providing personal space and encouraging individuality and better quality relationships. (Wolfensberger, 1972). There is no automatic guarantee that the drive towards 'community-based services' will provide these.

These changes are essential to help people with learning difficulties to develop and mature as individuals. There is now an increasing number of services with improved practice in Britain showing positive results. But services are still very patchy. Instances of full participation in decision-making and major life choices are still rare despite the general acceptance of those principles.

Real participation in decision-making will occur more easily if we concentrate on improving interpersonal relationships. Our services continue to place the majority of people with learning difficulties in relationships which hinder personal growth and development and restrict their ability for full participation. A plethora of traditional barriers exist - shift systems, duty rotas, bath books - as well as constipated notions of professionalism which hinder freer and easier relationships.

The traditional segregated services produce mostly poor interaction for people as contact between staff and clients is infrequent and of poor quality. However, research (CMHERA, 1984) into small staff homes indicates that whilst the frequency of staff/client interactions was higher, the quality of this contact may not necessarily promote personal growth and development. To bring about the improvement in quality of life so

7

much needed by our clients it is essential to provide a secure foundation. Leisure activities for handicapped people living at home are still largely solitary and passive, mainly involving contact with parents and little with non-handicapped peers. As the majority of clients living at home receive segregated day services, their daily social interaction is largely on the client/staff, child/parent basis which limits development.

We can improve the quality of relationships by:

- Recognising that users have been part of a powerful devaluing process, damaging to their self image and development. People in our service may need additional help and support to discover their full potential. That damage may also affect us. We can become disillusioned, exhausted and part of the problem. Sucked into the 'greed of giving', we get some sort of perverted satisfaction out of helping handicapped people to become dependent on us, thereby infantilising them. They play eternal children to our pseudo parenting;

- Enhancing the level and quality of communication of our clients by seeing clearly through the negative experiences and the stigmata into the humanity of individual handicapped people. We need to explore and experiment with different levels and types of communication to overcome clients' difficulties with expression or comprehension, seeking specialised help when necessary;

- By really listening. This is immensely difficult, especially when someone's speech is slow and indistinct. By giving quiet time and space, they can control the pace. Concentrate on validation and affirmation. We all know how to listen to words but it is often difficult to 'hear' what people are saying. Communication can come even more eloquently through physical movements rather than words;

- By enabling people to talk and to relate. Perhaps they like to be active. Join in these activities, whether it's playing pool, gardening, football or sewing, and use the time to encourage personal growth;

- Making conscious attempts to be positive. In conversation, praise steps forward as much as possible; for example, take note of a passive individual who says 'No' for the first time. Some management systems are intensely devaluing of staff as well as consumers. Staff don't feel involved in major decisions concerning the running of the service; some systems actually hinder individual choices like, for example, bulk purchasing policies; some services are short of training and support facilities and have poor staffing ratios. In such circumstances, it is easy to feel disillusioned and overwhelmed.

Models of care heavily influence ways in which consumers are helped by staff. For years services have been moving away from a model of 'total care' towards one which promotes skills training and independence. This shift results from the recognition that old ways were adding to people's handicap by increasing dependency and perceived deviance from others.

Sometimes consumers are so handicapped that they need many things 'done for them'. Often there seems no good reason to 'do things' for people who can learn for themselves and yet the service persists in promoting dependency. That reflects a power relationship. Staff are 'doers', 'competent', 'responsible for'. Consumers receive the message that they are 'passive', 'not able to', 'not good enough to', helping to create an image of inadequacy affecting their general confidence in relating to the world.

This imbalance of power is evident even in so called 'good' services. In districts which have adopted Individual Programme Plans (IPPs) for clients as an essential part of the service, consumers are subtly discouraged from taking initiatives. The staff convene the IPP meetings and communicate in a hundred ways who has the real power. IPPs can become another way of colonising handicapped people.

Perceived competence in everyday skills promotes self images and confidence-assisting personal growth. However, skills training can simply reflect the unequal power relationship between staff and consumers. If the number of instructions given in residential settings and ATCs were counted, who would mostly give them to whom?

Most of us experience a wide range of human relationships. In some we are relatively powerful; in others relatively weak. We have people who love and 'look after' us and we also care for others. We have people we teach and people we learn from. This constant shift and the width in our relationships is vital to gain a balanced perception of ourselves as valued individuals. People with learning difficulties, however, are most frequently at the less powerful end of interpersonal relationships, which leads to a very imbalanced view, a poor self image, which can stunt per-

9

sonal growth.

Services are moving gradually away from a quasi-parental model of caring towards a model based on more brotherly/sisterly relationships, relationships with many more facets. We need to narrow the social distances between staff and consumers so that more easy going relationships, bordering on and including friendship, can emerge. That means more sharing of our lives, more respect, liking and loving. Staff will need much help and support to work towards those sorts of relationships. Existing systems often make them more difficult. There are complicated regulations about using private cars for taking consumers in; professional courses often train students in the stiffest of relationships. (Mansell, 1986).

An important development in recent years has been befriending schemes. People with learning difficulties have very little experience of relating to non-handicapped people except in the role of relative or client. Those roles have tended to be rather narrowing and stiff. Most non-handicapped people with whom they mix who are not relatives are usually social workers, ATC staff, doctors, who are paid to be with them.

Isolation is a great problem for handicapped people living in the community. 'I 'aint got nobody. I'm one on my own. I don't get no visitors. There's nobody to talk to. I'm like one of those chocolate misshapes.' 'I am lonely. That's why I go out walking in the early hours. I can't sleep...everyone needs a bit of company now and again.' (Wertheimer, 1985). Handicapped people often have few allies living locally. They are not likely to be part of any valued old boy or girl network. You meet more powerful people at the Rotary Club or Golf Club than at the ATC bingo evening. We all need influential friends and supporters.

The main emphasis of befriending is on sharing rather than helping. Befrienders are people who are not paid to spend time with people with learning difficulties, to go to the cinema, funfair, church, restaurant, or on holiday with them. Hopefully, the befrienders get pleasure from spending time with a handicapped person they like and respect. These people can be anyone - greengrocers, neighbours, friends of relatives....

In an informal sense, befriending can help meet some instrumental and expressive needs. Instrumental needs include solving practical and material problems; advice on day-to-day issues like shopping and transport. Expressive needs mean providing emotional support during stress and crisis; maintaining sympathetic communication; bringing friendship; sharing in activities like meals and football games; sending birthday cards, giving Christmas presents.

Befrienders are enabling their friends to build up a bank of experiences; to develop social skills; to widen their social network. They provide a human gateway into the community, allowing their friends with handicaps to explore.

Paid staff have a major role in developing befriending. Consumers often have few skills in forming those kinds of relationships. They may be too 'shy' or 'come on too strong'. The service needs to welcome incomers of all kinds. Settings have to be provided in which non-handicapped people can meet consumers in warm and positive situations. Staff need training in working with volunteers of all kinds to prevent jealousies and rivalries emerging. It is necessary to avoid training which attempts to incorporate befrienders subtly, as part of agency provision.

Another important development has been in advocacy. The term self-advocacy has been used to describe encouraging handicapped people to speak for themselves, to express their needs. (Williams and Schoultz, 1981). Citizen advocacy is where a volunteer represents a handicapped person. (National Citizen Advocacy, 1989).

Self-advocacy can enable handicapped people to take more control over their own lives. Sometimes that has meant groups of handicapped people getting together to form self-advocacy groups like People First. Most groups have an advisor who is not there to control but to give advice when asked. (CMH, 1988).

For individuals, it means being encouraged to make more decisions. That involves professionals having a sense of 'realistic optimism' that handicapped people can and should take more control over their own lives. That requires a basic and powerful assumption that handicapped people are responsible, adult citizens. People need a lot of encouragement to perceive themselves as people of real value after years of denigration.

This involves risk. Bob Perske (1988) writes of 'the dignity of risk'. People learn from making mistakes as well as from getting it right. It may mean some social skills training, particularly help in learning to be assertive after years of informal training in being passive. They need practice in saying 'No'.

Citizen advocacy involves representing handicapped people through one to one volunteers: one volunteer advocate to one handicapped person. There is a considerable and necessary element of befriending in the relationship but here the advocate may often be in conflict with the service providers. It is important that the advocate's loyalty to the handicapped person is not compromised in any way. He or she must feel free

11

to speak out. Citizen advocates are appointed and supported by an independent agency not connected organisationally or financially with those providing the services. (O'Brien, 1987).

Nowadays, there is a positive explosion in counselling and psychotherapy and a blossoming interest in the field of learning difficulties. But is it any more than a passing fad, fashionable for a short time and then forgotten ? Hopefully, it is part of a general humanising of services. Whether it turns out to be a genuine healing process, helping restore our wholeness, can only be judged over many years. There are immense and largely invisible dangers - the dangers of Godgame. Therapy can be the biggest power trip of all. To be sardonic, the whole development of counselling and psychotherapy can be a process of psychopaths earning a living from the wallets of neurotics!

Another danger is that counselling systems will simply adjust people to what is, at best, a superficial society and, at worst, a vicious, destructive and untruthful one. Another is that we will learn a series of techniques around psychoanalysis or behaviour therapy or transactional analysis which will bring a little stardust to ourselves and the customers but have no effect at all on the wider structures. My pet hate is a social skills package. Some skills courses are rarely about real life. The ultimate test must be, how real is it? Can you bite it with your teeth?

Listen to this cry from the heart. 'Our deficiencies and unmet needs are the ore and coal of the service industries. Thus, the servers called teachers need students. But as their raw material declines, as the baby boom drops off, what do they do? How can they justify their work in the same numbers as the child population decreases ? One answer is to 'discover' new, unperceived, unmet needs - or the need for 'life-long learning'. ....The service economy presents a dilemma: that is the need for need. A million people (in the USA) each year move from goods to service production; the service industry requires more raw material - more need. We can now see that 'need' requires us to discover more human deficiencies.

'....We are in a struggle against clienthood, against merely servicing the poor. We must reallocate the power, authority and legitimacy stolen by the institutions of our society. We must oppose those interests of corporate, professional and managerial America that thrive on the dependency of the American people. We must commit ourselves to reallocation of power to the people we serve so that we no longer will need to serve. Only then will we have a chance to realise the American dream: the right to be a citizen and to create, invent, produce and care'. (McKnight, 1980).

Already we see the creeping growth of that substantial industry. We are beset by a jungle of newfangled jargon. Suddenly, the phrase 'challenging behaviours' flourishes like poison ivy in every book and pamphlet. 'How to deal with challenging behaviours'. She is 'expressing verbal aggression' rather than she is 'angry'. For the former we are already stretching for the sedative; in the latter we are forced to ask why she is angry. Psychotherapists have the highest suicide and breakdown rate of any profession. Physician, heal thyself! It is not hard to be a plastic guru, flying like Icarus with waxen wings too close to the sun. That results in a bloody mess. It is much harder to walk than to fly. So far, what has occurred in the fields of learning difficulties and mental illness cannot help us feel optimistic. In mental illness, therapy has rarely led to liberation but, at best, to new ways of adapting and, at worst, to even more sophisticated methods of control.

Counselling with people with learning difficulties can be the full flowering of human ordinariness. It can help devalued and marginalised people feel much more human, valued and worthwhile, able to cope with the ordinary sufferings and joys of life. Like everyone else, they will feel rejected, become bereaved, get depressed. Many still have to discover that they matter as human beings in a world which uses terms like 'subnormals', 'defectives' and 'spas' and 'divis'. The more disabled our clients are, the more we will have to use methods which don't rely primarily on verbal content. Loquacity and articulateness are not only different but practically opposites. Many people whose vocabulary is comparatively restricted can describe clearly what is happening to them, whereas more loquacious people get lost in a fug of words and ideas.

We may touch a lot in our work, often the most intimate expression of contact between human beings. We shake hands at first meeting and on departure, place an arm on the shoulder when someone is distressed - such gestures should 'feel right' to you or they will probably feel 'wrong' to the recipient. When we want to convey being 'moved' by someone we often say 'we were touched'.

Playing out a real situation can often be helpful. For example, if someone wants to explore a problem with a parent, it can be acted out. It can be much more powerful to act out an argument between a parent and a son or daughter than to discuss it. Systems like psychodrama or dramatherapy can be moving and enlightening. Laughter is just as liberating as crying.

None of this should devalue the importance of spending time in the development of ordinary ties and friendships. It helps us to learn about people's real lives: to walk a little distance in their mocassins. Drawing a picture of the way days are spent can often tell us a great deal about how handicapping and boring some people's lives are. They spend most time waiting for something to happen and in the invisible grip of powerful others.

Counselling is a process involving two or more people, one person listening and the other talking - simple but not easy. We are learning to gain increased respect and knowledge of one another. If it works, they should gain increased personal value, feel less threatened by others and become gradually more open and loving. That process has little to do with so-called intelligence.

At its best, counselling can be a powerful help. It tries to provide security for growth, to let wounds and damage heal. It allows us to listen to people's stories and look at the pain and joys of ordinary living. At its worst, it provides yet another oppressive human service.

Counselling must have good ingredients, like a winter warming broth. The basic ingredient of all good counselling is attention. We need to put the other person's head on our shoulders and feel how the world seems to them.

Coping with distressed people is not a question of how much you know or read, but of listening and seeing. Your own courage, warmth and vitality is the best asset. Your own experience of depression and despair can be a major asset if used wisely.

Here are a few basic rules:

- Keep communication simple.
- Listen to your own body as well as watching what is happening to the other person. If they are struggling to use an unfamiliar emotional language, then body movements will be an even more important means of expression.
- Try to stay quiet within yourself. Discipline your body by sitting reasonably upright and keep your breathing slow and regular and your speech even and unhurried. Say things in another way if what you have said is not understood. If you have nothing to say, say nothing. If you really cannot cope, find someone who can.
- Try to be both positive and concrete. Realistic optimism is desirable. Assume you don't understand what the other person is experi-

encing. Respect their wisdom. Avoid judgements about what they should or ought to have done or be doing.

- Stay in the present time. Concentrate on what the person is doing and saying. When your concentration wanders, bring it back. Note whether the other person is tired or finding it hard to concentrate and have a tea or coffee break or end the session.
- Listen carefully to the colour of the communication as well as the content. Note the feelings which bubble up as well as the words.
- Give people space and time to say what they want to say. Don't hurry or hustle.
- Be straight. Avoid doing things, like telephoning others, behind their back. Don't play games like jollying people along with 'never mind' or 'you'll be alright.' If you don't know something then say clearly 'I don't know.'
- Never be afraid of bringing in people with more knowledge and experience if that is fine with the other person.

Remember, next time it could be your turn...

References

Anderson, D. (1982) Social Work and Mental Handicap. Macmillan.

Brandon, D and **Ridley, J**. (1985) Beginning to Listen. CMH.

CMH (1988) Learning about Self Advocacy. (LASA pack: five volumes).

CMHERA (1984) An Evaluation of an Adult Residential Services.

Hollins, S. and **Grimer, M.** (1988) Going Somewhere. SPCK.

Ivan Illich, (1975) Medical Nemesis. Boyars.

Mansell, J. and **Porterfield, J**. (1986) Staff and Staff Training for a Residential Service. CMH.

McKnight, J.L. (1980) Social Services and the Poor: Who Needs Who? Public Welfare, Washington, USA.

National Citizen Advocacy (1989) Citizen Advocacy - A Powerful Partnership.

O'Brien, J. (1987) Learning from Citizen Advocacy Programs, Georgia. Advocacy Office, USA.

Perske R. (1988) Circles of Friends. Abingdon Press

Wertheimer, A. (1985) Housing: a consumer perspective. CMH.

Williams P. and **Schoultz, B** (1981) We can Speak for Ourselves. Souvenir Press.

Wolfensberger, W. (1972) Normalisation. National Institute on Mental Retardation.

Chapter 2

Slings and Arrows

David Barron

The main reason I started writing the books, the four volumes of my life history, was because I had so much pain and suffering to work through. It was like a voice inside my head which nagged for years, 'You've got to do something.' I'd been locked away for more than 20 years in a mental institution as a mental defective. By writing it all down I felt I could work it through my system and perhaps others could benefit from reading it. I wanted to stop this ever happening to anyone else.

I was just over eleven years old on first admission to Whixley mental hospital near York. This is what I wrote about it.*

'After taking one glance round the ward I knew there and then I did not like it. The place seemed more like a prison than a ward and in one sense of the word that is more or less what it was as I was about to find out. The attendant in charge took me through two rooms which were both locked. He had to unlock the doors then lock them again behind us. It was a case of wherever you went a bunch of keys was needed before you could gain access. The attendant took me through to a bathroom and even that was locked.....All the windows had bars'.

Whixley was a place of severe discipline. Bathtime was no exception. On bathdays, 30 or 40 of us crammed into one small room with a radiator with a guard round it. We all stood with a towel wrapped round our waists, sometimes for as long as an hour, standing on a cold stone floor, even in winter. It was freezing. There were only six baths in the whole place.

Eventually came the bath. 'Right, son, drop your towel and put your hands in the air,' the attendant commanded. When I carried out this humiliating order, he examined me from top to bottom with a big magnifying glass. 'Bend down now and touch your toes.' That was to ensure there were no vermin. 'Right, son, you can get into the bath.'

Another ritual was the Sunday walk. It was called the chain gang or the Whixley crawl, marching through the quiet country lanes. More than four hundred patients all lined up, all different shapes and sizes. The Superintendent walked down the lines, like a military inspection, to see we were all reasonably smartly dressed. We did exercises before the walk. Another part of the Sunday ritual was compulsory Church services, held in the large dining hall. We were made to participate in sports like football and cricket.

Violence was common. I recall being hit many times by both patients and staff. I went up to an attendant who was speaking to somebody and when I interrupted he just smacked me around the mouth. 'You speak when you're spoken to and not otherwise.' I saw a lot of violence. The usual punishment for speaking at the dining table was scrubbing a concrete yard with a common housebrick. Patients would frequently rebel against this. They would throw the bucket over the railings and often the brick as well. Attendants took them into siderooms. I saw three or four beating up one patient. They were using fists and putting the knee in. He cried out in pain, 'Why don't you come at me one at a time?'

It was impossible to win. The Superintendent always held the ace card. He could send people to Rampton State Institution at Retford. Most people sent there never came back. I was sent there for six months. I was punished for failing to stand up when the Superintendent came round the wards. It was really terrible in Rampton. Everything was terrible. Attendants didn't know the meaning of words. They just used their fists on everybody. They were trying to make sure that if I went in like a lion, I came out like a lamb.

The whole place felt like being in a cage with wired netting around the living quarters. You felt like a wild animal. The food was terrible. Most was uneatable and you were lucky to get half a slice of bread. You had just a bare mattress to sleep on. When attendants beat you up they used the cold towel method, both in Rampton and Whixley. They soaked towels in cold water and hit out with the wet coil. Sometimes they placed the wet towel on your body and punched through it so not to leave any bruising. It was like a medical compost.

Sexual abuse was very common. It was nothing fresh to walk down the ward and see an attendant in bed with a patient - committing sexually indecent assaults. I was raped by both staff and patients alike shortly after admission. I was a young boy amongst adults. There were beasts in that hospital.

Ward 1 of Whixley Hospital

Gateway to Whixley Parish Church. Coffins were brought from the hospital for burial at the back, separate from the main burial ground

David Barron

ONE

MY NAME IS DAVID CENTH BARRON
i WAS BORN ON AUGUST 10TH 8/ 1925.
IN BACHELER STREET LEEDS 2.
MY MUTHERS NAME IS B:TRUS MAYBUL
BARRON. FORMLY CHAPMAN. MY THATHERS
NAME. IS NOT NOWN, I HAVE NAVER SEEN
MY MUM AND DAD. BUT IT IS NOT FOR,
THE WONT OF TRINS
    I CAME OUT OF THE ORTHNIDJ ~~SÆT~~ THE ᴬᵀ
AGE OF 5 YEARS. AND WAS PLAYST IN THE
CMRE OF A FOSTER MUTHER. TERND OUT ᴴᴼᵂ
TO BE A CARDISTIKT. ONE. ~~AT~~ AT ~~WE~~
THE AGE OF E 11½ YEARS. I WAS
TACKON A WAY FROM MY FOSTER,
MUTHER. AND PUT IN FO A MANTUL
HOSPITUL. WICH THE A FORÓTIS SAID,
WAS TO BE MY NEW HOME. AND THAT,
I WOULD BE WEL LOOKT HATHTER · AND,
THAT I. WOULD GIET THE BEST OF ~~TREETMN~~
TREET. MANT . THAT WAS TO BE THE
UNDER STAYTMONT OF THE DAY AS i WAS
A BOUT TO FIND OOT. AFTEAR T.HE,
FORMIERTIS ~~AND HAD BE~~ OVE MY j
HAD MISHON. AD BEEN. KONPLEETID,
THE 2 MEN WICH HAD TACKON ME,
THERE LEFT. I WAS TACKON DAWN TO,
WARD ONE. THE A TENDUNT PULD OUT,
A BIG BUNCH OF KEES. UNLOCKT, HE
THE DORE LET ME IN. WOT A SHOK,
IT WAS FOR ME AS I STOD AND LOOKT,
A RAWND. WARD DORS LOCKT &
BEIND ME. WINDWS WITH BARS UT,
AT THAM. AND IF THAT WAS NOT BAD
IEE NUTH. I WAS TACKUN UP STARS,
AND TOLD TO STREIP OF AND FOLD AL

Extract from 'A Price to be Born' in David Barron's phonetic script.

20

MY KLOWS UP. I WAS THEN GIVON,
A NIHT SHERT ~~AND THEN~~ AND THEN
TOLD TO GO IN TO THE ROOM. AND
THEN THE BIG HION DORE WAS,
SLAMND AND LOCKT BE IND ME.
~~IT KONSISTID~~ THE ROOM KONSISTID,
OF ONE BED. AND A CHAMBER POT,
A SMAL WINDOW WITH BARS UP ~~AT IT~~ AT IT,
i JUST LAYD ON ~~THE~~ MY BED,
AND KRID MY ICYS OUT HAS HALI,
KOOD SAY TO MY SELTH WAS WOT,
HAD I DON TO DEZRV THAT AND THE,
MORE I FORT A BOUT IT THE MOR I,
KRID UNTIL I KRID MY SELTH TO SLEEP.
HATHTER TAYKING ONE GLANC,
RAND THE WARD i NEW THER AND THEN,
i DID NOT LICK iT. THE PLACE CIMD MORE,
LICK A PRISON THAN A WARD AND IN ONE,
SINS OF THE WARD THAT iS MORE OR LNYS,
WOT iT WAS HAS i WAS A BOUT TO FIND OUT.
THEE A TENDONT IN CHAJ TOOK ME THORW TOW,
ROOM'S WiCH WERE BUF LOCKT.
HE HAD TO UNLOCK THE DOR'S THEN LOCK,
THAM A GAYN BIND US. iT WA A KAYS OF, ~~WERE~~
                              BUNCH
WERE HETHER YOU WHENT A ~~BUNCH~~ OF KEE'S WHERE,
NEEDID BEFOR YOU KOOD GAYN HAKSES. ~~THEY~~
THEE ATENDONT TOCK ME THROOW TO A BATH ROOM AND,
HEEVON THAT WAS LOCKT. WRIT HE SAID SET,
UNDREST SUN. HATHTER i HAD DUN SO HE PONTID TO A SAYT,
OF SCAYL'S WRIT SUN JUST SET ON THOW'S SCAYLS. i WONTTO,
SEE HAW MUCH YOU WAY. HATHTER RECORDING MY WAYT IN A BOOK,
HEE HEG SAMIND ME FERERLY FROM TOP TO TOW'S THAN HE,
TOLD ME TO SET INTO THE BATH WHEN THE WOTER WAS TO HAWER.
                                                   MUST
MUCHERL SATIS FAKSHUN HE SAYT A BOUT BATHING ME. HE HAVE,
FORT i WAS IN KAYPERBUL OF BATHING MY SELTH

21

Once, I asked for some writing paper and envelopes. 'Come up to my room and have some chocolate,' said the attendant. There was a room at the end of each dormitory where the night staff stayed overnight. I went to his room and he was standing in a short shirt. I knew what was going to happen so grabbed the chocolate, envelope and paper, rushed out, took the keys and locked the door.

It was an awful life inside the hospital although I knew no other way of living. You never knew when some sadistic attendant would beat you up; you were dumped in the punishment ward for the smallest reason. You never knew when an attack would come from a patient; you never knew from one minute to the next when they would force sex on you.

What helped me to keep sane more than anything was helping others. I helped other patients to help themselves. If a patient had his left shoe on his right foot, I changed it round. I cared for people in practical ways. In the occupational therapy department, where they had epileptic fit cases, I worked as an unpaid assistant instructor. Some of the patients had the minds of children but all needed real love and understanding. The patients in there loved me and I loved them. They put trust and faith in me.

You never leave these things completely behind you. Others won't let you. When I left Whixley Hospital, I had three things to face: coming out of a mental institution; that I couldn't read and write - didn't know the difference between A and B; and my tremendously strong urges. I was getting urges to do to young children what had been done to me. If any man walked round the streets and did those things to children which were done to me - over and over and over again, against my will - those children would grow up and do them to other children. The only answer for me would be suicide. I tried to end my life several times.

I had got married but couldn't relate to my wife sexually at all. We weren't happy together. The marriage was annulled on the grounds of cruelty on her side. She led me a life of hell. Through all the pressure I collapsed. I was working as a porter in a Manchester Hospital and was taken into Bridgewater Hospital. I tried to take my life by taking lots of pills. It was a criminal offence at that time. Before I was taken to court the specialist put up two pictures of a male and female and asked, 'Which of those two would affect you the quickest?' I pointed at the man.

Shortly after the hospital offered drug treatment for my urges. They told me that they couldn't offer any guarantees but the drug might take my urges away. I accepted quickly, anything was better than what I was going through. The drugs had side effects; for example, my breasts became painful and swelled up. It was embarrassing in the swimming baths. People would say, 'Oooh, you're like a girl....' But it was worthwhile. I was so happy that young people could come into my home. I can now walk the streets without fear of anything happening to anyone.

I started to work at the Curzon cinema in Urmston, and I wanted to keep my brain functioning properly. Now there was a different urge - to get things on paper, to tell my story. I was clearing out all the terrible things of the past, instead of dwelling on them. By writing I could get away from the nightmares - about the fists, the beatings, the sex and the sordid filth going on. Without the writing I would have gone mad. I used to get up at eight in the morning and began printing out page after page on old exercise books in a phonetic script. I had taught myself this with some help. I would often go on for twelve hours or more, month after month.

It was all like seeing a film. It came into my mind. I would go to bed at night and wake up with a feeling that some particular event I had described was not exactly right - just like a film. I had the wrong sequence or someone had said something slightly different to what I had written. So it was all altered.

I did detective work to get things right. I went to a fête held at the old Church in Armley, Leeds, which I used to attend and someone gave me photos of how it was when I was a child. I got permission from the social services to go around an old people's home. It used to be Armley Grange Open Air Special School which I attended just before admission to Whixley.

The biggest search was trying to trace my real mother and father because I had been fostered out whilst still very young with a woman who was an absolute sadist. A lady in a post office told me she knew where my mother was living in Leeds. Someone came to visit and asked for my birth certificate and gave me an address not far away. I got dressed up in a new suit and looked smart.

I went with a friend by bus to a flat above a shop. Eventually, a lady came down and asked me who I wanted to see. I said I'd come to see my mother. She got all hot and bothered. I was getting upset. I said, 'I don't want you to think I'm trying to gain entry to your house under false pretences. I am who I say I am. I'm looking for my mother.' Eventually they let me in.

It turned out that the birth certificate I had wasn't mine. It had on my birth certificate David Frederick Barron: Mother - Beatrice Mabel Barron formerly Chapman. Their son came home and was very angry and yelled and swore until he settled down. We weren't getting anywhere so I left eventually. Later I got another birth certificate which read David Kenneth Barron: Mother - Beatrice Mabel Barron formerly Chapman. The more I think about it, the more convinced I am that in that hour or two, I made contact with my real mother.

As part of the detective work, I went back to Whixley Hospital. I was nervous but memories came flooding back. After the first volume came out in 1981, I was received with open arms. They did everything but put down the red carpet. I lectured to some student nurses. I went round and took photos. But when the second book came out, which is purely about my time in the hospital, the staff were hostile. I was writing critically about people they knew - friends and relatives.

The books gave me a chance to tell my story. I told the whole truth which stopped me getting bitter about people. People can learn from it. The books helped because through them, I've made true friends. For example, I met the co-author of my books. He is a postman. I saw him once a year to give him a little something at Christmas. I invited him in one day to look at my work. He took away my phonetical notes and re-wrote it in proper writing and spelling. Nowadays, I go to his home one week and he comes to mine the next.

I got to know my good friend David Barker, a lecturer at the University of Manchester, through the books. He had been trying to track me down through hearing of the books through the articles which had been in the paper. Now they are my family.

I've still got my memories and the pain. I sometimes find it hard being alone after so many years of being with others, never having to think for yourself, doing what you were told.

I've got to watch I don't slip back into institutional ways. They are hard habits to get out of and I still cling to some routines. We were compelled by institutional laws to turn our beds down. Every bed was turned down completely and the Superintendent or attendant in charge of the ward, went down with a line and everything had to be straight. To this day, in my little flat, I still turn my bed down, ready for inspection!

After all these years I'm still damaged. I'm afraid to go out at nights. I'm afraid in crowds. The books have helped clear my system. Uncovering my story has helped keep me alive. The books got me into places I would otherwise never have got into. I lecture in colleges, which helps me as well as the students, and I get articles published in local newspapers. It's lovely that people show interest in my life.

* Enquiries about David Barron's four volumes of his life history, A Price to be Born - Twenty Years in a Mental Institution, should be addressed to David Barker, Department of Social Policy, University of Manchester, Oxford Road, Manchester M13 9PL.

Chapter 3

Understanding Emotions

Nigel Beail

A prevalent view among professionals is that psychotherapy has no place in services for people with learning difficulties. This view is now being challenged. Through historical and social changes, in particular, reforms in children's education and the recognition that everyone is educable, we are becoming aware of the emotional needs of people with learning difficulties. Like everyone else, they have 'an inner world as well as an outer one, an unconscious as well as a conscious, and therefore need just as much access to psychotherapy as others.' (Sinason, 1988a).

Throughout history services for people with learning difficulties have been dominated by one model or another. For years segregation and incarceration were the vogue. The medical model only seemed to rationalise what had gone before. The current fashions are normalisation and behaviourism. Behavioural approaches have advanced both the service and the quality of life for people with learning difficulties. Unfortunately, it has become too dominant to the exclusion of other approaches. Behaviourism is not a panacea and when professionals looked for alternatives they found a limited literature. Basic texts on psychotherapy make little or no reference to people with learning difficulties. When they do it is usually in the form of exclusion criteria (for example, Bloch, 1979, Brown and Pedder, 1979). Although one of Bloch's criteria for people to undergo psychotherapy is that they should be 'at least of average intelligence', he also points out that research on criteria for psychotherapy has yielded little of practical value and its impact on clinical work has been minimal. No research has been done to relate criteria to people with learning difficulties so 'at least of average intelligence' has no validity. There seems to be an assumption that lack of intelligence makes the individual an emotional cripple. As Sinason (1988a) points out, 'however crippled someone's performance intelligence might be, there still can be intact the richness of emotional structure and capacity.' Psychoanalytical psychotherapists should not be concerned with people's level of intelligence but try to help improve their emotional quality of life as well as overcome their emotional problems.

Psychoanalytic psychotherapy seeks to expose the defences (denial, regression, repression) clients use to deal with their anxieties, and the underlying unconscious impulses and emotions. Mental life is a function of the interplay between several aspects of the mind - the id, the ego and the superego. (Freud, 1923). These are fuelled by two main instincts - life and death. The life instinct aims to establish greater unity and the death instinct tries to destroy.

The id is a receptacle for unacceptable, repressed experiences and memories. The ego tries to preserve the self - dealing with both the internal world of the id by controlling the instincts and the external reality. The ego strives after pleasure and seeks to avoid pain - one of its major activities is to repress painful experiences into the id.

The ego also has the task of simultaneously satisfying the demands of the superego, a psychological system where the demands of parents have been internalised. It contains a punitive aspect as well as a more positive ego-ideal. The ego and the id correspond roughly to the conscious and the unconscious and the superego to the conscience.

My approach has its roots in Freudian theory but is heavily influenced by the work of Melanie Klein. (1975).

When someone is referred to me it is usually because their relatives or carers are seeking help for unwanted behaviour or symptoms of anxiety or depression. Psychoanalytical psychotherapists view such unwanted behaviours or symptoms as end products of mental mechanisms. The behaviour or symptom has an expressive as well as a defensive function, containing the avoided feelings or impulses in a disguised form. The main task of the psychotherapist is to analyse in his or her mind and then interpret to the client the end product of these mental mechanisms in terms of: (a) the devices adopted for avoiding pain, conflict, or unacceptable feelings (the defence); (b) the feared consequences of expressing these hidden feelings (the anxiety); and (c) the nature of the hidden feelings. (Malan, 1979).

Wherever possible, clients should be seen in a therapy room rather than at their own home. Michael, the subject of my second case study, could not be seen at my place of work because of his fear of leaving his house and his parents. His parents had no transport and lived in an area poorly served by public transport so I saw him at home. This impeded therapy as Michael has persecution anxiety and was in constant fear that his persecutors (his parents and neighbours) were listening to us.

The therapy room should be light, warm and comfortable, if possible with an alternative choice of seating - a couch for the client to lie on or comfortable chairs. In either case, the therapist and client should not face each other - clients find it easier to talk about certain things when they are not facing the therapist. The physical setting, appointment times and frequency should remain constant.

Central to the process of therapy is the therapeutic alliance. To foster such a relationship the therapist needs to be respectful and non-judgemental. Anna Freud advocated that in child analysis, the child had first to become attached to the therapist. Similarly, Bowlby notes the importance of a secure base (a temporary attachment figure) from which the person can explore. The therapist allies himself with the client's conscious ego against the split-off parts of their nature. He offers himself as a partner, earning confidence and trust, laying the foundation for a working alliance and transference.

Transference refers to elements of distortion in the client's perception of the therapeutic relationship. More loosely, it refers to any feelings the client may have about the therapist. Clients experience feelings towards the therapist as if he or she were a significant person from a past or current relationship. In my work with people with learning difficulties, I have found that little effort was required to facilitate transference. It clearly operates, as Klein states, from the start of therapy. Parsons and Upton (1982) found that the relationship rapidly becomes very intense. They suggest that this may be because many people with learning difficulties rarely have the experience of someone just being with them and trying hard to understand the communication.

Transference is one of the main tools of the psychoanalytical psychotherapist. Transference provides clients with an opportunity to work through their needs, wishes and reactions to other people over and over again in relation to the therapist. Together, we examine more closely and safely the defence mechanisms which have lead to the building of inner worlds and distorted perceptions of reality.

Counter-transference is the feeling of the therapist responsive to the transferred feelings of the client. These are important because they may stem from the therapist's conflicts and impede his or her ability to understand and result in deviation from treatment. The therapist may also feel the same way as other people in their client's network. For example, he may feel that the client is manipulative and then discover that so does the GP, the community nurse and the social worker. Supervision is extremely important for psychoanalytical psychotherapists as the therapist has to work through his or her own feelings.

In psychoanalytical psychotherapy, clients are encouraged to say whatever comes in to their minds, however silly or upsetting. This is called free association. Three main types of intervention are used - *confrontation, clarification* and *interpretation. Confrontation* draws the client's attention to what they appear to be doing, often repeatedly and seemingly unconsciously - for example, blaming themselves for everything. *Clarification* helps sort out what is happening by questioning and rephrasing. *Interpretation* refers to all comments and other verbal interventions which aim to make the client aware of some previously unconscious aspects of their psychological functioning.

In using free association with people with learning difficulties, I found that a considerable amount of the material presented came in the form of experienced urges and impulses encapsulated in phantasy. Often, clients are unable to distinguish between phantasy, dreams and reality. These phantasies were also strongly sexual, aggressive and sado-masochistic in content. Greater emphasis is given to phantasy by Kleinian theorists. Kleinians view phantasy-forming as a function of the ego and they see a direct relationship between instincts, phantasy and mental mechanisms. Susan Issacs (1952) put forward the view that our instincts are expressed through phantasy. Our phantasies have unconscious content. For example, through phantasy we satisfy an instinctual urge by an appropriate object. This implies that the ego is driven by instincts and anxiety to form relationships in phantasy and reality. Kleinian theorists are concerned with how phantasies relate to the reality of the outside world in the way it has been experienced in the past and in the present.

Something which puzzled me very early on was how material which usually took months or even longer to access in clients who did not have a learning difficulty was much easier to access in those who did. This suggests that there is easier communication between the conscious and unconscious in the minds of people with learning difficulties. However, such material was presented in ways which protected clients - it was somehow separate, with all the bad things about an experience contained elsewhere, in others. To defend themselves against conflict or anxiety stirred up by an experience, clients were not repressing these experiences as we would expect following Freud's theory. My clients used a number of other defence mechanisms described by Melanie Klein. (1975). She outlines four central mechanisms which operate before repression - splitting, projection, introjection and projective identification. In splitting, the ego stops the bad part of an experience or self contaminating the good part, by dividing it, or it can split off and disown part of itself. In projection, the ego fills someone else with split feelings and experience. In introjection the ego takes into itself what is perceived in someone else or an experience. In projective identification, the ego projects part of itself into someone else with whom it identifies - becoming like the person it has already imaginatively filled with itself. Splitting, projection, introjection and projective identification are the main defence mechanisms I have observed in clients. Other defences include denial and idealisation. I have not found much evidence of repression.

....

JOHN

John is 26 years old and lives with his mother and stepfather. He had been living at home since he left school. He was brought to the attention of the local mental handicap service by his parents because he had become 'disruptive'. John was hitting his mother, staying up all night, 'banging about' and not respecting anyone's privacy. He talked all the time asking repeated questions which, because of his slurred speech, were mostly indecipherable. He was admitted to hospital to give his parents a break. They wanted him to leave home but there was nowhere to go. He was referred to me for a 'behaviour modification programme'. I saw John and offered to see him weekly to see if I could help. He was now back at home and attending a psychiatric day hospital. At the day hospital he built space ships and insisted that he take them outside and take off. This behaviour created considerable consternation for the staff who did not feel he should attend the day hospital because he was mentally handicapped and they were not trained to deal with such people - a sad reflection on specialisation.

In the early stages of therapy John seemed to be experiencing great pressure to speak. The sessions were very intense with John asking questions and demanding answers. My initial interpretations concerned his feelings of being constantly anxious. In response to these interpretations, he told me about a childhood experience. Two boys had sex with him. They were bad boys and it was a horrible experience. As therapy progressed, John brought more and more in the way of dreams and phantasies to the sessions which he demanded I explain. Here is an example:

John: *There are some alien boys.*

Me: *What are they like?*

John: *Look similar to earth boys - they wear space underpants - futuristic underpants.*

Me: *How many boys?*

John: *As many as the planet can produce - twin alien boys.*

Me: *Why twins?*

John: *To swop places with earth twins. I will be the emperor and a twin boy and have it off with earth boys. I would have it off with all the alien boys. The boys would be recruited for space armies and they would have sex with me. I would offer them sweets to have sex with me, if they wished to have sex it would be alright. I wouldn't force them. This would be a special breed of boys like bees from larva growing in cocoons on rocks, developed without females - just from boys. I will have it off with boys from 9 to 13.*

Through exploration and interpretation of his dreams and phantasies it became clear to John that he enjoyed part of the sexual experience with the boys and then experienced guilt. He protected himself from conflicting feelings by splitting off the bad and guilty parts and projecting them into the two boys - they were 'bad boys'. However, in his phantasy, he is the abuser. Freud (1895) argued that the 'psychical trauma (of abuse), or more precisely, the memory of the trauma, acts like a foreign body which long after entry must continue to be regarded as an agent still at work'. In John's case, the 'agent' is still at work in his phantasies some 17 years later. Sinason (1988b) comments that 'Freud was aware of the repetitive nature of abuse', and Klein's later comments (1932), that guilt itself heightens sexual desire and causes further disturbed sexual behaviour, is also linked to Freud's idea (1923) that guilt can itself cause a crime. In John's case the crime of abusing other children took place in phantasy. This sexual theme continued throughout John's three years of therapy.

John's mother and stepfather had requested that he move into some form of residential care. In sessions John would not talk about his mother or respond to any interpretations regarding their relationship. That she wanted rid of him was too painful a loss to bear. His anxieties were being communicated through his activities at the day hospital. The space ship symbolised himself and the earth his mother and taking off being the threat of separation and expulsion into the unknown and unsafe world. In his phantasy, he defends himself against this by living in a world where women are not required. He is the emperor, in total control and has omnipotently triumphed over women. Klein traced this configuration of defences back to the time when as infants we discover our dependence on mother. To defend ourselves against the fear of losing her we deny our dependence by becoming omnipotent through phantasies of controlling and defeating the mother. John is mobilising these defences in facing a fear of loss and abandonment.

This extract is from a therapy session which took place during the sixteenth month. John's mother still wanted him to leave. His speech had improved considerably but was still slurred and at times rushed. To understand what he was saying I asked him to repeat and slow down. I did not record these interventions and they are not in the following transcript. The session was 50 minutes in length and ran over by a further 15 minutes. However, the transcript is quite short. John was familiar with the method of free association and started the session by telling me about a dream he had that week.

John: *I had a nightmare. I dreamt about going back into hospital. Started with an ambulance arriving at my house. They wanted Murdoch but they took me instead. They put me in there. There is a nurse there, and two nude men who were getting ready to go to bed - unattractive men, like other patients at that hospital who are a bit mad. Nurse said 'What are you two doing with no clothes on? Get to bed.' Then we went to bed and it was the next day and they took me by ambulance to our old house and they let me out because they hadn't got Murdoch. Then a car came. It was like true to life. They came in the house and went off again.*

Through the dream, John communicates his two main anxieties: his fear of separation and his anxieties regarding his earlier sexual abuse.

Me: *How were you feeling when they brought you into the hospital?*
(Clarification)

John: *Alright. There must be some reason for bringing me into hospital.*

Me: *You said it was a nightmare, but that it was alright?*
(Confrontation)

33

John: *It was a shock to me.*

Me: *You fear being admitted to hospital again?*
(Interpretation)

John: *Yeah.*

Me: *You don't feel as well as you think you should?*
(Interpretation)

John: *In what way?*

Me: *You feel you are going mad?*
(Interpretation)

John: *No. I've not gone mad, but I have got a different sense of humour - we have all got a different sense of humour.*

Me: *You are not feeling very safe at the moment?*
(Interpretation)

John: *That's true.*

Me: *You feel your Mum wants rid of you?*
(Interpretation)

John: *That's true - it's her anniversary today with stepfather.*

Whilst accepting my interpretation, John immediately showed resistance by trying to change the subject. So I repeated the interpretation in relation to his step-father.

Me: *He wants rid of you too?*
(Interpretation)

John: *It's alright at the moment. We are trying to cope with each other - OK?*

John increased his resistance and denied the problem so I restated the interpretation adding that it evokes painful feelings.

Me: *These feelings that your Mum wants rid of you - that must be very painful?*

John: *Yeah. What were those two nude men? Not getting dressed. What does that mean?*

John increases his resistance even further by returning to the dream. At this point I put my interpretation on the back boiler.

Me: Is that something you've seen before?
(Clarification)

John: *Yeah.*

Me: *On a ward?*

John: *No. With Andrew and David.*

Andrew and David are the two boys who had sex with him when he was a child.

Me: *So Andrew and David are still popping into your dreams?*
(Clarification)

John: *Yeah - as different people in different positions.*

This illustrates how an earlier experience which caused him so much anxiety which he defended himself against still manifests itself in dreams 17 years later.

Me: *When you came onto the ward and saw them, did you think they were Andrew and David?*
(Clarification)

John: *They didn't look like them.*

Me: *They made you think of Andrew and David?*
(Interpretation)

John: *Yeah - their nudeness.*

Me: *You felt sexually attracted towards them?*
(Interpretation)

John: *Might have done.*

Me: *So you say that they were unattractive but had some sexual feeling there?*
(Interpetration)

John: *They reminded me of Andrew and David in the nude.*

Here, John denies the part of him that felt sexually excited by the incident. So I developed the interpretation to include the part of him that feels guilt.

Me: *Andrew and David still make you feel excited but at the same time you feel guilt and shame?*

(Interpretation)

John: *Yeah. It's 10.30 now.*

John was pointing out that our 50 minutes were up. Perhaps he saw this as an opportunity to resist further exploration of his sexuality.

Me: *You want to end?*
(Interpretation)

John: *No, we've got something else now.*

Suddenly, John became very anxious and his speech rushed.

John: *I've still got sexual feelings and have dreams about having it off with men and boys. Will it go away?*

Me: *You want it to go away?*
(Interpretation)

John: *If you can get rid of it.*

Me: *You think I have the power to get rid of it?*
(Interpretation)

Here, John's fantasies about being a powerful person are being projected onto me.

John: *No, not really. I have two sexual feelings, one to men and one to women. You make the decision of which one to have.*

Me: *You feel you can't have both?*
(Interpretation)

John: *No. I have to have one or the other. I feel I might make the wrong choice.*

Me: *You must feel very confused?*
(Interpretation)

John: *Yeah.*

Me: *Lonely?*
(Interpretation)

John: *Yes, lonely. No sexual partner.*

Me: *You can't have a sexual partner because you can't decide what you want?*

36

(Interpretation)

John: *I want a partner.*

Me: *You want a partner?*

John: *I have tried many ways of getting a partner. I go to a club, church, to see if I can get a girlfriend.*

Me: *So you want a girlfriend?*
(Interpretation)

John: *Yeah.*

Me: *But you also like boys?*
(Confrontation)

John: *I look at boys and wish I was younger.*

Here was an opportunity to restate my earlier interpretation.

Me: *You wish you were still Mummy's little boy?*
(Interpretation)

John: *I wish I wasn't ageing so much.*

Me: *You would like to feel that your Mum still wanted you at home.*
(Interpretation)

John now lets out some of his anger.

John: *I wish I had a better education and life. I wish I was born in the future and all this being me wouldn't have happened. This is not the right period for me. There is nothing for me on this planet. I wish I was born later.*

Me: *You feel you don't belong?*
(Interpretation)

John: *I am far ahead of everybody.*

John defends himself against his anxiety by becoming omnipotent and then feels safe to end the session.

John: *We'd better stop now. Can I go and get a cup of coffee?*

Me: *You want to stop?*
(Interpretation)

John: *Yeah. When's my next appointment?*

MICHAEL

When Michael was referred he was 28 years old and living with his parents. All three were unemployed. Michael had had a long association with the psychiatric and mental handicap services and the social services but all agencies had withdrawn except for a community nurse who popped in every few months. I had to see Michael at home as he did not like leaving the house and could not travel on buses. The main problem for which help was sort was Michael's cross-dressing. However, during my first few sessions with him, it was abundantly clear he felt overwhelmed by intense aggressive impulses.

A typical outburst was: 'I hate people. I want to murder. I want to kill people. I'll kill him with a sledge hammer. I'll knife him.'

He also felt persecuted by his parents, particularly his mother. 'They hate me. They've turned against me. She wants to hurt me. She's got evil in her. She's wicked - she's making me like it.'

These feelings extended to people in the neighbourhood: 'Nobody likes me. Everyone's against me. They pick on me. No one likes me round here.'

During sessions, Michael would tell me to 'Shut up - someone's out there. Be quiet, be quiet'. He would go and look outside the room several times. At other times he would tell me that 'everyone is frightened' of him and that he has 'threatened to beat him up' or 'I'm going to get that woman and give her a right good hiding'. Then he would tell me that 'people aren't teasing me any more. They say 'hello' in the street. I talk to people now I'm friends with everybody'. But this was usually short-lived and he would demand: 'You've got to stop me going round the street telling people to f... off'.

Michael also frequently became hypochondriacal: 'I'm getting pains in my chest.' 'I ache all over.' 'I'm constipated.' 'My stomach's on fire.' 'I feel sick and get indigestion.'

Sometimes he felt he wanted to die, or was dying. 'I keep thinking I'm going to die.'

He had numerous obsessions, such as touching medicine bottles and bottles of cleaning fluid. He became violent at home to his parents and to household objects. He also threatened people in the street.

Michael presented a challenge to his environment but also to my approach. He did not respond to the initial interpretations so I analysed the massive amount of material he was providing to see how I could most appropriately respond to his needs.

Michael's feelings of hate were the manifestation of the death instinct. From the beginning of life we try to deal with the conflict between the death and life instincts by modifying the death drive with the life drive or by expelling the death drive into the outside world. Michael coped with hateful and aggressive impulses by splitting them off and projecting them into his parents and other people.

His parents and others were seen as being full of hate. He felt persecuted by them - they hated him. He could not expell all his aggression. He identified with his phantasized aggressors and consequently through introjection felt full of hate again, not only his own hate but the phantasized hate of others. This led to hypochondriacal symptoms - pains and other manifestations which in phantasy resulted from the attacks of the hate of others inside him against the ego. If someone was nice to him, then everyone was good and he felt better. But this was short lived as the phantasy is fragile and easily destroyed by a negative event. For example, a young boy passing the house spoke to Michael in a friendly way as he stood in the garden. Michael went out to find other children to play with. He tried to join the game of football but they told him to clear off. He hated everybody and everybody hated him. In Michael's world, you are either good or bad - you cannot be both.

Michael's own aggressive feelings were also reinforced by the introjection of his parents' relationship, characterised by hostility and violence. In introjecting his parents, he filled himself with bad things to add to his own instinctual feelings of hate. He desperately attempted to keep the good parts of himself and others separate from the bad parts. By projecting the bad parts into the external world, he felt persecuted.

This splitting of good and bad is violent and excessive. Within a single session, people switch from being good to bad and back again. Such excessive splitting and projective identification weakens the ego and thus the person is unable to assimilate his inner feelings and feels ruled by them.

My attempts to interpret did not produce a response in terms of clarity or relief. Michael would just continue to bombard me with more questions. Klein (1946) observed that splitting processes can account for this failure of contact between client and therapist and lack of response to intepretations. The defence mechanisms of splitting, projection, introjection and projective identification can dominate any other form of communication. Perception of inner and outer reality can become so distorted that normal communication is impossible. Michael's parents also complained - 'You just can't talk to him'.

As interpretation of free associations was not working, an alternative treatment approach was necessary. In the course of my work, I have noticed that with some clients it is not clear at times who is talking to me. I made this observation in Michael's sessions. He would speak to me like his mother and complain of the same physical symptoms as his mother. He was taking his mother's clothes and dressing up during the night. He told me of his phantasy of his father finding him dressed up and beating him. (His father had a history of wife beating). Michael would never stay in on his own at home. If one parent left the room, the door had to be left open.

When I saw Michael with his parents before and after sessions, he would bombard them with questions and accusations, provoking hostile reactions. He was also incapable of doing anything without asking. I hypothesized that Michael did not experience himself as a separate individual. He did not know what was him and what belonged to others. Steiner (1979) shows this confusion as a consequence of excessive splitting and projection.

Mollon and Parry (1984) point out that psychoanalytic theorists generally accept that a sense of self as a separate individual is not given but is an outcome of a slowly evolving process - the gradual emergence from a state of primary identification with the mother. Michael seemed to exist, in part, in this state of primary identification, or felt cruelly pushed out of the maternal space and was attempting to regain the right to reside there.

How can someone like Michael be helped? The therapist is constantly bombarded and confronted with questions charged with anxiety and demands for reassurance. Our gut reaction is to provide reassurance. But would this be right? Malan (1979) argues that the therapist must bring out anxieties and trace them to their origin, not drive them underground through reassurance. I felt an overwhelming temptation to offer reassurance but took Malan's advice. Driving Michael's anxieties underground would mean further splitting and projection. What Michael needed was a 'container' to keep his attention and allow, momentarily at least, parts of his personality to be held together as 'concretely as a skin' (Bick, 1968).

Therapy had to enable Michael to feel secure as a separate individual. In normal development, this requires the mother, and subsequently the family, to provide a safe base from which the person can explore and to which they can return. Through exploration, the person develops a sense of separateness, an identify and sense of self, distinct from the mother's or family's. Kohut (1971) argues that during this time the child depends on the presence of admiring empathically responsive or idealized others. These are felt by the child to be part of himself and provide a stepping stone to a more separate psychological existence. In Kleinian terms, the child takes in (introjects) the good objects and strengthens the ego. As more and more good objects are introjected, the child feels better about himself and that others respond to his love. Klein (1959) felt these experiences contribute to a stable personality and make it possible to extend sympathy and friendly feelings to others.

Michael did not feel separate. He felt persecuted and full of hate. My role as therapist required the provision of a containing environment in which he could discover the limits of feelings of love and hate, a place where he could express feelings without retaliation or negative consequences. I accepted his anxieties as real and acknowledged that feelings and behaviour were important and had meaning for him. So, when he bombarded me with questions about cross-dressing, I accepted that need and encouraged him. Gradually, there was a reduction in anxiety as he explored feelings about wanting to cross-dress and how he felt when dressed as a woman. When he said someone was 'against' him, I accepted that and explored the reasons. When he said, 'Have I just taken a bottle of tablets?', I would reply, 'Do you think you have?' The usual response was 'Of course you haven't. Don't be so stupid'. Michael had come to call these feelings his 'silly ideas'. I suggested that he may feel they are silly but that doesn't mean he is silly and that these feelings also have some important meaning.

Therapy provided Michael with predominantly good experiences and he began to introject some good feelings and experiences into himself. In fact, he gradually began to idealize me - I became the source of all good things. 'I can talk to you', 'You are going to make me better', 'You can sort it out', 'I feel much better when you're here. Can't you come more often?' This idealization enabled me to allow Michael to experience gradual disillusionment with me - I couldn't come more often, I didn't have a magical cure - thus enabling him to see good and bad in one person. I could encourage him to make choices and decisions by reflecting his demands.

It was a painstaking process. After twelve months of therapy Michael still made intense demands but only during the first part of a session. As a session progressed, the demands and persecutory anxiety subsided and he became calmer. He felt more secure and separate. He stopped borrowing mother's clothes and bought some of his own. He could stay on his own for short periods and he had fewer 'silly ideas'. He started to talk about leaving home and getting a job. In later sessions, it was possible to use interpretation to slowly unravel the intricacies of his early and continuing introjection and projections.

....

Conclusions

For Michael, therapy continues but John terminated after three years. By that time, he had left his mother and was living in a small hostel. He had also resolved conflicts regarding his sexuality. He had been treated unsuccessfully with drugs and his parents would not accept a behavioural approach suggested by a colleague. We worked through painful and conflicting emotions and he now has a better quality of life.

These two case studies illustrate how psychoanalytic-psychotherapy can be used to help someone with a learning difficulty who has problems. In John's case, I worked with him on dreams and phantasies by suggesting meaning through interpretation, clarifying his experience and bringing relief. This approach did not work for Michael. For him an important factor was not interventions such as interpretation but filling early developmental needs (Winnicott, 1965), a sort of developmental second chance (Greenberg and Mitchell, 1983). Change did not take place through interpretation but through experience and this enabled us to progress to introducing interpretation.

References

Bick, E. (1968) The experience of the skin in early object-relations. International Journal of Psychoanalysis, 49, 484-6.

Bloch, S. (1979) Assessment of patients for psychotherapy. British Journal of Psychiatry, 135, 193-208.

Brown, D. and **Pedder, J.** (1979) Introduction to Psychotherapy: An Outline of Psychodynamic Principles and Practice, Tavistock, London.

Freud, S. (1895). Preliminary Communications, Hogarth Press, London.

Freud, S. (1923) The Ego and the Id. Hogarth Press, London.

Greenberg, J.R. and **Mitchell, S.A.** (1983) Object Relations in Psychoanalytic Theory. Harvard University Press, Cambridge, M.A.

Issacs, S. (1952) The nature and function of phantasy. In: Klein, M. et al (ed). Developments in Psychoanalysis. Hogarth Press, London.

Klein, M. (1932) The sexual activities of children. In: The Psychoanalysis of Children.

Hogarth Press, London.

Klein, M. (1946) Notes on some schizoid mechanisms. International Journal of Psychoanalysis, XXVII, 99-110.

Klein, M. (1959) Our adult world and its roots in infancy. Human Relations, XII(4), 291-303.

Klein, M (1975) The writings of Melanie Klein, l: Love, Guilt and Reparation and other works; II: The Psychoanalysis of Children; III: Envy, Gratitude and other works; IV: Narrative of a Child Analysis. Hogarth Press, London.

Kohut, H. (1971) The Analysis of Self. International Universities Press, New York.

Malan, D. (1979) Individual Psychotherapy and the Science of Psychodynamics. Butterworths, London.

Mollon, P. and **Parry, G.** (1979) The fragile self: narcissistic disturbance and the protective function of depression. British Journal of Medical Psychology, 57(2), 137-146.

Parsons, J. and **Upton, P.** (1982) Psychodynamic psychotherapy with mentally handicapped patients: technical issues. Paper presented to the British Psychological Society Annual Conference.

Sinason, V. (1988a) Psychodynamic psychotherapy and its application. Paper presented to the Forum on Mental Retardation. The Royal Society of Medicine, London.

Sinason, V. (1988b) Smiling, swallowing, sickening and stupefying: the effects of sexual abuse on the child. Psychoanalytic Psychotherapy, 3(2), 97-111. ˜

Steiner, J. (1979) The borderline between the paranoid-schizoid and the depressive positions in the borderline patient. The British Journal of Medical Psychology, 52(4), 385-392.

Winnicott, D.W. (1965) The Maturational Process and the Facilitating Environment. International Universities Press, New York.

Chapter 4

In Tune with the Mind

Margaret Heal

'Music is a miracle.'

William made this comment spontaneously during a music therapy session after 20 minutes of improvisation on the piano. This boy had been sexually abused and struggled to communicate a mixture of conflicting emotions. His music provided a multisensory means of expressing these emotions - anger, excitement, guilt. As a music therapist, I witnessed and facilitated his exploration of feelings.

'Music makes me feel sad, especially now because a holiday is coming.' John had suffered neglect and deprivation from an early age. At school, he was seen as the happy fool, the smiling idiot, oblivious to the world around him. Music therapy offered a holding space where he could begin to feel emotions that were painful and dangerous.

I told George that a holiday was coming up so we wouldn't see each other for a while and asked about his feelings. 'I was get angry on the bus I was. Yeah, Andrew throws shit on me.' I responded, 'Music is about being able to be angry.' Though his response was not directly about me, he used another situation to express his feelings about the impending break - a change from the violent reactions he often acted out. He had found words to express how he felt about me leaving - I was throwing shit on him.

Music therapy helped William, John and George to become more aware of their emotions and offered a creative way to communicate.

The Association of Professional Music Therapists (1986) describes music therapy as providing '...a framework in which a mutual relationship is set up between client and therapist. The growing relationship allows changes to occur, both in the condition of the client and in the form that the therapy takes. By using music creatively in a clinical setting, the therapist seeks to establish an interaction, a shared musical experience leading to the pursuit of therapeutic goals. These goals are determined by the therapist's understanding of the client's pathology and personal needs.'

The Association goes on to stress that 'the therapist must be a highly skilled musician capable of musical creativity with clinically directed aims. Music therapists also need to develop an understanding of their own reactions and responses as well as those of their clients so there can be a growing awareness of the many and various aspects of the therapist/client relationship.' The music therapist must be able to move other people emotionally through music: to communicate emotions musically for and with the client. The main musical technique used is musical improvisation: 'Any contribution of sounds and silence spontaneously created within a framework of beginning and ending'. In a music therapy session, this is called clinical improvisation: 'Musical improvisation with specific therapeutic meaning and purpose in an environment facilitating response and interaction.' (APMT, 1985).

Within this definition of music therapy, each therapist finds a way of working suited to his or her character, temperament and personal style. As a new profession, we develop our own theories about the relevant dynamic processes. However, it is necessary to borrow from other disciplines to further our understanding and my work is informed by psychoanalytic theory.

This approach necessitates firm therapeutic boundaries: sessions are held in the same room, at the same time each week and are protected, as far as possible, from interruptions and intrusions. Holidays are prepared for and their effects taken into account. It is through using these boundaries that a musical frame can be provided in the same 'hello' and 'goodbye' songs each session. The same choice of instruments is always available.

I try to understand the meaning the sounds, verbal and non-verbal, the movements, and the musical instruments have for the client, as well as for the developing relationship between the client and myself. These observations are made in the context of the sequence of events in the session and this sequence is compared with previous ones. I attempt to understand and communicate the therapeutic issues or themes explored in the session.

Sinason (1986, 1989) describes some therapeutic issues which are more apparent in work with people who have learning difficulties. There is the grief the person has experienced over having 'lost the normal selfhood she or he would have had without a handicap'. Mourning is continually experienced throughout life: 'Leaving school but not for 'real' college; leaving home but not for real independence; living in a group hostel but not really sharing a flat.' She discusses 'the envy of normality and hatred of workers that can be hidden under 'smiles' and false over-friendliness.' There is the use of the state of mental handicap to defend against dealing with a traumatic event (for example, sexual or physical abuse) or the real extent of the learning difficulty. 'Being the village idiot is a way of hiding the extent of the handicap and making fools of the staff and the population who wish to court the view that handicapped people are friendly and have nice smiles.'

How can these issues be further understood through the use of the elements of music during clinical improvisations in music therapy sessions? Let's look at the elements of pitch, intensity, articulation, tempo and rhythm, and the possible meanings they could be given:

- Pitch has a different feeling, depending on how high or low it is. For example, a high sound can feel tense, whereas a low sound which has a slow vibration that can be felt in the instrument tends to be more comforting.
- Intensity or volume can be used. There can be a need in some clients to play loudly, to drown out the thoughts and feelings they and the therapist are having, to remain out of touch and 'stupid'; a need in others may be to play softly, perhaps showing a fear of speaking out or being heard, to remain unnoticed, unseen.
- The articulation or touch of a drum being banged abusively is different in feeling (and meaning) from one being tapped gently.
- What meaning does playing at a fast tempo or speed hold for a client with learning difficulties who knows intimately the label 'slow'?
- If a client plays in a staid, repetitive rhythm, or lacks any rhythmic cohesiveness, what does this say about the way he or she is able to deal with the external world?

The client's difficulty in improvising to feel a natural beginning, middle and end may have a similar meaning to the client in psychotherapy who has difficulty in tolerating the ending of each session and the holidays which interrupt the sequence. This is related to the ability to deal with endings, separations and feelings of grief.

The choice of instruments is important. Why would someone choose to blow a recorder rather than strum a curvaceous guitar? As well as shape and the way an instrument is played (struck, blown or strummed), the timbre or quality of the sound is important. Imagine the difference in feeling between the jingling of bells and the beating of a drum.

The two case studies I have chosen illustrate some of these elements. The setting is a special school for adolescents with severe and moderate learning difficulties.

GEORGE

George is 14 years old. He appears a happy boy, offering a large welcoming smile. At five years old, he was assessed as having severe learning difficulties. However, on the insistence of his parents, he was placed in a school for children with moderate learning difficulties.

He was referred for music therapy by his class teacher who was worried by his behaviour. George could be self-abusive, head-banging or hand- biting. He would deny having made unprovoked, spiteful attacks on other children witnessed by the teacher. The teacher found himself struggling to understand the communications George offered. George is verbally able but seems to live in a world of his own. For him, this internal world is the only real, safe one.

George was offered a half-hour individual music therapy session on a weekly basis. The boundaries of time and place were maintained throughout the five terms of therapy. He quickly chose his favourite instrument, the piano. Other instruments he chose to play during various sessions were the timpani drum, the guitar, the tambourine, and the twin Chinese cymbals which were suspended from a music stand.

George's sessions were fast moving, frantic outpourings of sound and movement. The early sessions were particularly confusing. 'Miss, listen to this...' George banged the big drum with one hand as he played clusters (groups of notes) on the piano with the other. 'My cousin has a drum, the big one. My Dad walks like this..' George imitated on the piano the sound of his father walking. 'Did you see the film? Nice film. What's it called? Nice film. See the train on the grass. Nice film. My bus has two buttons like this. Listen, this is a nice one.' George imitates in the bass (low part) of the piano his bus backing up.. 'My driver is my friend...'.

I found myself faced with the tasks of a mother: to find a way of holding and accepting the seemingly chaotic flood of sound and movement exploding from George, making it manageable for him; and to help him link the thoughts and feelings inside himself with what went on outside. I wanted George to experience a successful mother and baby duet.

At the beginning of the sessions, we would both sit in front of the piano to play and sing the 'hello' song. In the early sessions, George would make a direct line for the chair positioned in front of the bass area of the piano. The 'hello' song would soon be drowned in a series of low pitched atonal clusters (groups of all different notes, like hammering your fist on the piano) that were banged out in a hoppity-skip rhythm. It was impossible for me to support him, to provide a foundation and much needed structure for his chaos.

I decided to insist on having the chair which he sat in. By moving him into the treble (high part of the piano), I was allowing the opportunity for the mother and baby duet to happen. Whether or not he wanted this was another matter. When I asked him to move, he smiled a compliant smile and sat in the chair in front of the treble.

George improvised in the treble, atonal clusters with the same repetitive hoppity-skip rhythm. I tried playing solid, open sounding chords with a similar rhythm in the low range of the piano. George would either stop playing his rhythm and bounce his hand across the notes into my territory or begin to tell me an exciting story with no connection to what we were doing. If I tried to respond verbally to his music or stories, my words would be lost in a torrent of sound, crashing clusters on the piano or repetitive beats on the drum. George seemed to be afraid of any interaction outside of him which he could not control. Intimacy was dangerous.

I decided to add some new sounds to his musical vocabulary at the piano, rather than talk about what he was doing. He seemed locked in the rhythm and behaviours he used. When he began bouncing in my territory, I answered with a glissando (sliding the hand up the keyboard, playing all the notes in succession quickly) in my area of the piano. His response was an amazed, 'Hey, how do you do that?' Perhaps this mother could be useful after all!

George was then willing to play at the same time as me, though not necessarily together, ending each improvisation with a glissando. George had been given a new way to stop the playing. Each session we would have several attempts at playing together. For a few seconds, we might lock rhythm, but soon George was running faster than ever, managing every time to beat me to the end of the duet!

I described George as the happy boy. I soon came to feel how much pain lay behind this 'happiness'. George told me a story: 'Oh, no.. he's slipping... someone tripped him... he fell down the stairs... we all laughing!' He accompanied this with appropriate sounds on the piano. I responded, 'Oh, that must have hurt.' George replied: 'Funny is happy!' What humiliating, painful situations had he endured to become the happy, laughing boy?

How could I link the feelings of the boy being tripped down the stairs with the powerful glissando George? An opportunity soon presented itself. George was upset by someone who had kicked him on the bus. He came in with his happy 'hahaha' expression on his face and began to bang out loud aggressive music on the piano. The incongruity between his facial expression and the music he chose to improvise was startling. How could I help him to connect his thoughts with his feelings, thus allowing him greater control of his actions? I put the sustaining pedal down and asked George to feel the vibrations resonating through the piano. I said, 'An angry piano, feel the anger.' Though George quickly changed the activity, the anger had been recognised and allowed.

During one session George began to play games with me. He would say, 'Look up, look down,' and proceed to attempt to hit me on the chin, saying, 'Caught you out!' He asked me to close my eyes while he proceeded to hit me on the head with a drum beater. The message was loud and clear: it is not safe to trust people, they will abuse you. I only let myself get caught in these games once. I had to be a protecting, safe mother. George was not allowed to abuse me.

The improvisations carried this same abusive feeling. We would play together as we had in past sessions. I would try various styles of accompaniment: open, sustained chords in the bass to provide a holding structure for his frantic outpourings; play one supportive chord with every four of his hoppity-skip bits; or just quietly listen. Whenever we played together, George would end his glissando on the highest note of the keyboard, point directly at my nose with his index finger and say triumphantly, 'Caught you out!' I felt angry every time, as if I was being abused. This helped me understand how he felt.

I asked him, 'Who catches you out?' George banged with a loud fist in the bass. I repeated the question. George responded by playing with both hands over the entire keyboard in his repetitive hoppity-skip rhythm thirteen times. This ended with seven loud hammerings of fists together on the piano. 'That's an angry George.' George replied, 'My brother.' I now understood. 'Your brother catches you out?' George slammed his fists down on the keyboard. I commented, 'And that makes you so angry.' The following session George ran a glissando from end to end of the piano whenever I began to play. Finally, I commented that he was playing in my half of the keyboard and that I couldn't play, so that I couldn't catch him out. The improvisations with a 'catch-me-out' ending began again. I found words to respond to this game: 'Sometimes you want to catch me out, to hurt me.' The 'catch-me-out' disappeared but the glissando remained to protect the ending.

George's Dad worked at the train station. George was always imitating fast trains, never slow trains. I realised that he had a need to play fast, to understand what 'fast' was about. Slow wasn't acceptable to him. I responded by commenting in a session: 'Some things are fast and some things are slow', and: 'There are all different ways to be, all different speeds.' Whether George was a slow train or a slow thinker, I would accept him. George could begin playing slower, less frantic improvisations at the piano.

I was surprised one session by the arrival of a puppy. George had knocked on the under-side of the piano. When I asked who was there, he yelped, 'A puppy!' George said the puppy wanted to be patted and showed me how to do this properly. I understood that the baby part of George wanted to be taken care of, wanted to be held and comforted. The puppy was always welcome to come out of the piano during sessions.

A few sessions later, another dog appeared, a Sally dog. Sally made different dog sounds, high yelping barks to low snarly growls. Whenever George talked about Sally, he called her he. I asked, 'Isn't Sally a girl's name?' Out of the piano jumped an aggressive dog named Tommy. I was beginning to understand the different characters that were in George, the parts he was struggling to hold in one mind, one piano.

It was at this point in the therapy, that I found a new job. I was leaving. To him, I was the abandoning mother. I felt terribly guilty, and yet I knew by providing a planned goodbye, I would help with future separations.

I told George I would be leaving and that we had four sessions left together. George turned the piano into a car. He used a drum stick in the piano lock as a key. George began to improvise and I joined in. He finished it with a glissando up the whole keyboard, through my territory. I commented, 'You don't want to need me to play.' George replied, 'Listen..' (He made sounds of a car being unable to start). I reflected, 'It won't start.' George passed me a small beater and showed me where to

51

tap the piano to make the engine work. I tapped it as I had been instructed and the car started. George imitated a car in perfect working order starting up. I commented, 'There it goes.' George asked to get inside the piano and see how the engine works. 'We can't get into the car.' The engine went dead again. It was difficult admitting to George that I didn't have the key to the piano. I was the inadequate mother who couldn't fix or change his brain, and the abandoning mother who was going away before the job was finished. 'I don't know how to fix it. Is it going?' George replied, 'No... finished.'

Later in this session George and I managed to play together, he on the guitar and me on the piano. He invited me to play with him and started us off, 'Ready, set...go!' We played together for thirty seconds matching rhythm and mood. George wasn't running away. The music came to a natural conclusion. George commented, 'Finished songs.'

I knew that in the final weeks it was important for me to respond beyond my own guilt and to acknowledge that George might feel afraid, that his engine wouldn't work without me. The following week George showed me just how much he didn't want to need me. He brought his own toy car from home and fixed it by ramming it with a drumstick from behind. I commented on how worried George was that he wouldn't be able to manage without me.

Throughout the five terms of therapy I had taped the sessions. George sometimes listened to excerpts from these tapes. I knew he understood that I was leaving when he was able to look at me during the last session and say: 'All the tapes are full.'

George's behaviour outside the sessions had changed over the course of therapy. He moved from being very self-abusive with head-banging and hand-biting, to externalising this anger and frustration. He was wetting his trousers and attacking other children. This was difficult for the classroom staff to deal with. He was given a support worker to watch over him at all times. Eventually, the violent outbursts disappeared almost altogether. His mother reported that George had begun to shout 'No' at home when he didn't want to do something. The school supported her in accepting and dealing with this new behaviour. George was now able to recognise his feelings of anger.

The music therapy sessions provided George with a safe place to explore the boundary between his internal world and the external world we shared. This distinction meant that he could then begin to externalise the anger he felt inside, anger which he had previously turned in on himself by hand-biting and head-banging. This boundary also meant he could defend himself from the feelings and actions of others. He could say, 'No!'

....

SUSAN

Susan is a chubby 15-year old with jet black hair and green eyes. Her medical record states she was born with a mild handicap. At the age of two years and two months, she had severe and uncontrollable epilepsy and had to spend prolonged periods of time in hospital. Her severe learning difficulties are seen to be the result of these early fits. She has not had a fit since she was three years old.

At the time of the fits, her parents were experiencing difficulties in their marriage. It is hard to say whether the marital difficulties came from the stress of having a handicapped child, or whether the fits were a response to the breaking up of the marriage. Her parents divorced and have since found new partners. Susan lives with Mum, her stepfather and new baby brother. Dad has one daughter from his second marriage. He doesn't see Susan.

Susan is obsessional and uses rituals to defend herself from the outside world and to control the feelings inside herself which seem all too powerful. Mum finds these rituals difficult to handle. All activities must be carried out in a certain order. If this doesn't happen, and quickly enough, Susan will have a tantrum. When Susan gets upset in public she will rip and strip off her clothes. Her tape recorder and tapes play a large role in these rituals.

Susan is also an elective mute. Though she rarely speaks at school, at home she has a vocabulary of 250 to 300 words. Her receptive language seems good. When a person is talking to her, she will avert her gaze or appear to be looking through you. She gets on well with other children at school, especially boys. She has a loud throaty laugh that will burst forth whenever she is amused, particularly when other children are being told off.

Susan came for music therapy once a week for twenty minutes. This was increased to twice a week after the first term. The time and place boundaries of the sessions were strictly adhered to. In the early sessions, Susan accompanied me tentatively to the music room. She didn't look at me. She would enter the room, pull a chair up to the drum, sit down, and pick up a drum stick. The electric piano was to her left. She stared to the

53

right. I performed songs for her and with her. She would beat the drum occasionally and sway in time to the music. We began each session with the 'hello' song.

I wanted to encourage interaction with Susan without being threatening. I started to talk to the drum which she felt secure with as 'Mr Drum'. Susan would beat loudly or softly depending on how she was experiencing my suggestions or commands. We were communicating through the drum.

Susan became enthused about attending music, walking quickly up the stairs and down the hall to the music room, a sharp contrast to the slow way she used to come. One session, I caught her eyeing the electric piano. 'Susan, if you want to play the piano, please join me.' She quickly moved the drum out of the way and pulled a chair up to the piano. Her playing at the keyboard changed over several weeks. At first she would barely sound the highest note on the piano. The territory she was willing to play in gradually increased down towards the middle of the keyboard. She would play random groups of notes with her favourite songs, swaying and looking directly ahead. Her playing became stronger and louder.

Susan seemed comfortable with the room and with me. It then felt safe to explore freer playing. After the 'hello' song and some playing of songs, I would leave time for Susan to experiment with the keyboard. This time gradually increased to the point that we were improvising through the entire session.

These improvisations were different from the improvisations with George. With George, I had been trying to provide some structure, some form for the chaotic sounds he produced, and to find some place that we could be together in the music. With Susan, the interactions involved the preverbal skills of turn-taking, imitation and initiation. Susan would quietly play a sound. I would then quietly respond with a sound or note and add another note to it, using notes on the keyboard or singing them. I was imitating and expanding on Susan's sounds, in a similar way that a mother imitates the sound of the baby and extends it to develop the sound vocabulary of the baby. The improvisations with Susan became quite raucous. She was using progressively larger groups of notes, and more and more of the keyboard territory. At times she would sing along or speak in airy, indiscernible words. Outside the music sessions, she was beginning to speak more. She had gone swimming with her class after one music session and had spent the time in the pool singing nursery rhymes with the other children. This had never happened before.

Though Susan was initiating sounds in music sessions, I did not feel she had tolerated imitating me at any time. I wondered how this related to her past experiences. What had she experienced between the age of two and three years, the time of the first autonomous steps? During this stage, children begin to experience that they are not omnipotent, that there is a world outside of themselves which they cannot control. Susan had experienced epileptic fits, prolonged separations from her parents in the hospital, and the breakdown of her family. Her words and behaviours

Perhaps it seemed safer for her to go I felt there was a need to link an airy voice, to the fast moving throaty laugh and a controlling to the sound sequence I had not omnipotent, that there was the imitation could be in pitch, rhythmically and pitchwise like a . There would be a feeling of d survive.

to meet Susan on a preverbal not feel compelled to hold her had begun to rework the early making once again the faltering dictable external world.

developed through the music. to provide a form for his chaos, his emotions. With Susan, the ful preverbal relationship. The ch bridged their internal worlds intimacy, the coming together hips is rewarding and painful. therapist that this transformations, there are no quick-fix solu-

so much, to Valerie Sinason and the rvision of my work, to Irvine Gersch

55

and Catherine Butler for their comments, and to my parents for their encouragement.

References
Association of Professional Music Therapists (1985) A Handbook of Terms Commonly in Use in Music Therapy.

Association of Professional Music Therapists (1986) A Career in Music Therapy.

Bruscia, K.E. (1988) A survey of treatment procedures in improvisational music therapy. Psychology of Music, l6(1), 10-24.

Heal, M.I. (1989) The use of precomposed music with a highly defended client. Journal of British Music Therapy, 3(1), 10-15.

Rayner, E. (1986) Human Development: An introduction to the psychodynamics of growth, maturity and ageing (3rd edition). Allen and Unwin, London.

Sinason, V. (1989) Working with handicap. Newsletter of the Association for Psychoanalytical Psychotherapy in the National Health Service, 5.

Sinason, V. (1986) Secondary mental handicap and its relationship to trauma. Psychoanalytic Psychotherapy, 2(2), 131-154.

Recommended reading
Alvin, J. (1975) Music Therapy. (Revised paperback edition). John Clare Books, London.

Alvin, J. (1976) Music for the Handicapped Child (2nd edition) OUP.

Alvin, J. (1978) Music therapy for the autistic child, OUP.

Boston, M. and **Szur, R.** (eds) (1983) Psychotherapy with severely deprived children. Routledge and Kegan Paul, London.

Boxhill, E.H. (1985) Music therapy for the developmentally disabled. Rockville, MD. Aspen Systems. Journal of British Music Therapy. Available from: Distribution Secretary, 69 Avondale Avenue, East Barnet, Herts EN4 8NB. Published twice yearly.

Nordoff, P. and **Robbins, C.** (1971) Therapy in music for handicapped children. Victor Gollancz, London.

Priestley, M. (1986) Music therapy in action. (2nd edition). St Louis, MMB.

Psychology of Music: a special issue on music therapy 16(1), 1988.

For information on music therapy, contact: Mrs Denize Christophers, British Society for Music Therapy, 69 Avondale Avenue, East Barnet, Herts EN4 8NB. Telephone: 01-368 8879.

Chapter 5

Humming Quietly

David Brandon

Work by myself and others shows that most people with learning diffi-culties feel the separation from ordinary people and the ordinary world, very deeply dislike being herded together on the grounds of so called si-miliar disability. However they have little say in the development of es-sentially colonialist health and social services.

Some conditions in Adult Training Centres come close to what else-where would be called slavery. Take this example from a 'trainee' in Scotland (Brandon, 1988). 'I've spent 18 years here. Nothing much hap-pens. I'm bored most of the time. Nothing to do. We play pool and domi-noes. I would like to earn some money and get out of this dump. The contract work for Johnny Walker, assembling cardboard boxes, is O.K. We make a thousand boxes and get an extra £2. That makes £4 a week. I like metal work, making boxes and running races in the Special Olym-pics.'

People are congregated on the grounds of handicap not because they are Zen Buddhists, Millwall football supporters or members of the Green Party. They are trained to behave in a disabled manner and to live a han-dicapped life. Most relationships are with relatives, paid staff and other handicapped persons. They have few substantial relationships with or-dinary valued non-paid persons. (Brandon & Ridley, 1985).

I have concentrated on teaching meditation to some people using an adult training centre because this is essentially a very valuing process, helping growth towards personal responsibility and maturity. I shared with them my experience as a Zen Buddhist monk and long years of doing and teaching meditation (Brandon, 1987). The great thirteenth century Japanese Zen teacher, Dogen, wrote 'There is no question here at all of being intelligent or stupid, nor is there any difference between the quick-witted and the dull. If you exert yourself singlemindedly, this is practising meditation.' The emphasis over many centuries has always been on devotion and dedication, not on high flying philosophy. The old Zen proverb states: 'Better than understand, simply experience.' It's simple but far from easy.

The ten weekly sessions were aimed at helping them to appreciate and value themselves in the negative and childish setting of an ATC. Our surroundings were saying silently that these people were really large children deserving little say in their daily living, who had to be told what to do. To his credit, the manager was aware that both staff and consumers suffered from long neglect and was working hard to undo negative processes. A massive county bureaucracy run by extremely well paid people considerable distances from ordinary users and staff did nothing at all to help.

I had met the staff a few weeks earlier at a meeting to explain about the meditation classes. All were curious, some enthusiastic, but others were sardonic and even actively hostile. One said, 'You're crazy to waste time teaching meditation to these people. It's far too difficult. They can't understand anything.' The atmosphere was largely agnostic except for one assistant who felt it was essentially a way of 'sneaking eastern religions in through the back door'. That was not one of the class objectives!

Numbers in our weekly groups varied between ten and fifteen: eight people attended all the sessions. Most people came from only two ATC classes, under the charge of two instructors favourably inclined. The group members had a lot of physical ill-health which explained most of the absenteeism. To relieve the considerable anxiety the atmosphere was kept light and humorous and an attempt was made to provide some security and validation. Most people began to feel safe after a few dodgy minutes.

I began by explaining what meditation was to a very earnest and nervous assembly of twelve people sitting in chairs in a circle. 'Meditation is about stilling the body as well as the mind.' With the amount of bottom twitching going on, I was in for a hard time! I asked whether anyone knew what meditation was. Everyone was either ignorant or too nervous to express an opinion. People just studied the floor with great intensity, quite understandable in the early stages of a group. I explained: 'It is a way of concentrating our minds on the present. There are a number of different ways of doing that and we're going to explore some of those together. We start this week with mantras.'

Much high quality rubbish is written about meditation systems using sounds, or mantras. A mantra is a repeated sound heard inside the mind or chanted over and over, out loud. It is essentially a very simple process to learn. I taught this group in about five minutes to get the feel of it. Their exploration was active and vigorous and their anxiety largely dispelled in ten tiring minutes. Perhaps this meditation stuff wasn't so difficult after all !

The group began with humming, getting louder and louder, until the noise gradually harmonised of its own accord. It began rather raucously and ended with a practised smoothness. They were delighted to hear the subtle harmonies and experience an unusual sense of power in working together. Until then they had seemed disjointed as a group. They were asked to feel the vibrations of the humming inside their own bodies and exaggerate the movements, expressing them all over the room. Soon, they became human tuning forks, moving all over the room like spinning tops. It was amazing the number of staff who found a reason to regularly pass our glass-paned door, particularly when the group was noisy. The corridor must have been exceptionally crowded !

After an hour of experimenting with various sounds, interspersed with several break periods and plenty of physical movements, contrasts between EEEEEs and OOOOOs and more kinds of humming, people seemed very relaxed. The change had been dramatic. They were asked to internalise the humming - to hear it inside the head whilst being silent. After a few minutes of help everyone succeeded, if only for a few seconds. 'It keeps going away. I get it but then it floats off. When I get it right, it's very nice but then it floats off.' I linked the experience of internal humming with dealing with disturbing emotions. I showed people individually how you could cope with anxiety through humming. Humming could be like a giant sponge, soaking up unpleasant feelings. It prevented the mind from fragmenting into pieces, holding it firmly together like cement. They practised the humming again and linked it with feeling distressed and overwhelmed.

For one person, that was a considerable revelation. 'I've never hummed before without humming. Just humming quietly inside my head. It quietened me down in no time at all. It's really great.' Another commented: 'At first it was a big struggle to get it and then it just came and felt good. When I get upset now, I can do my silent humming instead of scratching myself - red raw. Scratching gets me into trouble with Mum. She doesn't like it at all. She and my Dad tell me off and then I run away and cry and scratch myself again.' This vicious and destructive circle had gone on for years.

The session ended with simple relaxation exercises to taped music. This helped people to achieve states of mind without deliberate exertion. The music gives people permission to behave in ways considered weird in the ATC. It evokes the disco rather than the school. In an initial session with so called ordinary people, it would be death by ten thousand questions as people struggled to categorise the information they were being given, to relate it to what they already thought they knew. Meditation is always about giving up knowledge rather than acquiring it. Most people come to meditation groups with considerable baggage, especially about what meditation is or is not. They have read books and listened to tapes. There was none of that process evident in this group which made it considerably easier to teach the practice.

Everyone seemed to enjoy the experience and the time went very quickly. They had come tight and nervous and seemed to leave feeling more relaxed and valued. The favourable feedback to the staff helped our acceptance in the centre. Sessions had to be broken up into several segments to help sustain concentration. Perhaps because it involved lots of personal attention it seemed to give people a feeling of value. It had also been unusual, even a little strange, and there was an atmosphere of great energy and excitement in the room. One staff member enthused: 'People look different, more attractive and younger, more alive.' They chatted about the experience for days.

Sessions continued in the ATC for nine weeks. They had a set form, lasting just over an hour, which helped develop people's confidence. Now, they knew what was going to happen and had mastered some of the exercises. Staff said that people looked forward excitedly to the sessions. Wednesday became Meditation Day, even for people who didn't attend. Two staff were sufficiently interested to want to attend but the group decided firmly against that. 'It's only for us handicapped not for the staff. They can find somewhere else.' That seemed a wise decision as the staff had expressed interest in gaining another technique to use, like a Girl Guide or Boy Scout badge. 'I want to learn to do it to handicapped people' was one request. Meditation isn't 'done' to anyone.

People were encouraged to find a daily time for individual meditation practice - done away from our group. That raised tricky problems. Most people lived at home with parents and were usually heavily discouraged. Two lived in a local authority hostel and shared a bedroom with another person. All seemed to have little privacy and little control over their lives. One Dad said, 'You don't want to do strange things like that. It's not for the likes of you.' One group member was told firmly by his Mum, 'Meditation is too much for handicapped people. It strains their brains and gives headaches. You don't want headaches - do you ?' Some ordinary family homes were very controlling. Meditation was linked in many people's minds with high intelligence and reading the *Guardian* not the *Sun* or *Daily Mirror.* It was seen as extremely 'difficult', vaguely oriental and probably dangerous.

At the beginning of subsequent sessions, the group mostly practised the silent humming. It was familiar and comfortable. Later they went on to use a formal mantra. They used the sound PALI, PALI, PALI said rhythmically over and over. First, it was said out loud and then internalised with considerable ease. Their period of meditation practice, usually ten to fifteen minutes, gradually lengthened as the time went on. They found this a simple practice to learn after the experience with humming. These devices were a mental scaffolding to focus their minds on what was happening in the present.

Meditation based on visualisation was a rich area for exploration. A few people found this easier to learn than the auditory systems. Some people are more gifted at working with pictures than with sounds. We introduced it by using a number of brightly coloured balls. They were the brightest I could buy - vivid patterns of lines and circles in blues, reds and yellows. They symbolised fun and flexibility although I'm sure there were problems of age appropriateness !

The group concentrated on seeing the coloured balls in the middle of the table. They closed their eyes after looking intensely at them and tried to imprint the balls inside their minds. For many it was tiring. They tried this several times. After a few minutes the ball was spun very rapidly so the colours and patterns merged together. It was fascinating to see it whirl and the colours merge. They closed their eyes again and tried to see the ball spinning and spinning....

At one session we used soap bubbles which was very messy and did not please the ATC cleaners at all but it was enormous fun. We got into trouble with the Manager but it was worth it ! They blew multi- coloured soap bubbles with a very steady blow and watched until they burst. The slower and steadier the blow, the bigger the bubbles. Bigger bubbles were more exciting. They stared at the various colours on the bubbles and tried to see them with their eyes closed at the very moment of bursting. They were seeking energetically and fixedly for that single elusive moment and had to concentrate intently. They were learning about psychological fine tuning.

Sometimes we used a candle rather than balls or bubbles. The group would concentrate on the flickering flame for a few minutes and then try to see it with their eyes closed. For some that came easily. They opened their eyes several times to check the accuracy of their inner seeing. Eventually they could all sit for several minutes 'seeing' the candle in their mind's eye. Such exercises aid concentration immensely. 'When I first started I couldn't really see the candle with my eyes closed but now I can see it clearly. I just imagine it. It pops into my head - white wax, saucer and flame and everything.' Others would get into chronic 'I can't' strategies but with a little attention and finding alternative ways of doing it, they usually overcame initial negative reactions. The whole session was aimed at providing a positive and valuing experience, concentrating on achievement rather than on the pain of failure. Most members seemed to feel they were expanding and achieving in ways important to them.

Sometimes we used guided phantasies. They lay on the floor in neat rows and I told a story which they filled in with their own imagination and sense of adventure. It was teaching people to dream and have visions. Popular themes were 'My ideal house....' 'My ideal holiday....' It was both relaxing and stimulating.

Meditation on feelings can help unlock great potential. We sat as a group in the, by now, well established and comfortable circle. 'Close your eyes and breath slowly and deeply.' Close attention to breathing had become an established part of our practice together. They had learned to breath slowly and rapidly in different exercises. We played some relaxing music and asked them to picture someone they loved. For a few, with a background of institutional care, this was difficult and painful. Most chose Mum, a few Dad, and two a close staff member. We asked them to feel the love for that person come surging up through their bodies. I could see and feel the transformation taking place in the room. People just glowed with the warmth. One said, 'I felt a warm feeling in my stomach going through my chest into my head. It was lovely.' Another person said, 'I just wanted to cuddle everybody.' The love was being expressed profusely in the room and the group. It was very moving and softening.

Later sessions used robust meditational movements with lots of noise. These were a series of exercises, some stolen, from the martial arts, which were, at least originally, forms of meditation practice, and others from various sources like Hatha Yoga. They involved a number of themes - balance, grace, synchronising with explosive breathing and strength. They involve learning to be much more aware of the essential unity between body and mind.

People were involved in strange exercises steeped in fun. They forgot to be clumsy. They forgot their various physical handicaps and got on with it because there was no perceived understanding of what was excellent or poor. They showed wholehearted dedication. There is no way to do the exercises badly or well - you just do them with the whole of you.

We borrowed Kin Hin - a system of slow rhythmical walking - from Zen Buddhism. People enjoyed the slow and quiet walking around the large room in Indian file. For some, it was difficult to walk really slowly without falling over. They pretended to walk on a floor covered with thick treacle so it was sticky on the soles of the feet. If you walked really close behind someone else, it needed great concentration so as to avoid their heels ! If you failed in concentration, they yelled loudly. This slow walking delighted one person, who said, 'When I walk really slow, I can hear my real self better. It is much quieter and steadier than the rest of me.' This from a young lady who had been in and out of mental handicap hospital for her 'challenging behaviours'.

People who are handicapped have often been socialised into seeing their bodies as ugly and clumsy. 'Look at me, David. I can't do it. I'm just too clumsy. Got two left feet, my Dad says. Don't know my left from my right.' 'I can't do this. I'm just born awkward. My Mum says I tripped over my feet when born.' 'I'm just clumsy. I drop coffee cups all the time. Can't do anything without breaking or dropping it.' If taught sensitively, these movements can help people to feel and move gracefully and delicately, to feel more at ease with themselves and begin to uncover who and what they are. Dance and movements can help immensely in re-structuring body images. People can see themselves in a much more positive light. Sometimes their eyes glow. People are very diverse. Their minds vary enormously. Some visualise easily; others prefer sounds whilst others resonate more effectively with movements. Fortunately, meditation is thousands of years old and a vast treasure house full of different traditions and systems. Depending on the flexibility and knowledge of the teacher, something can be found for all in the treasure house.

However, it is important to practise what you preach. If you teach meditation, please do some yourself. There are few things worse than pseudo healers who don't take their own medicine! It is necessary to understand this particular medicine from the inside as well as the outside. There is usually an appropriate method or a combination which suits the person and that comes from long experience from many different methods and an absence of dogmatism.

People with learning difficulties have often been trained into seeing themselves as 'failures'. Often, they feel clumsy, lonely, unloved and unloveable They can't really succeed at anything considered worthwhile - can't get a paid job or go to a real school. They can't 'fail' at meditation. It is not about 'success' or 'failure'. It is about learning more thoroughly to be who we are already. Cleverness can be such a massive obstacle to wisdom.

References

Brandon, D. (1988) Report on an Occupational Strategy for People with severe learning difficulties in West Lothian, West Lothian Voluntary Council for People with Disabilities.

Brandon, D. and **Ridley, J.** (1985) Beginning to Listen, CMH.

Brandon, D. (1987) A Look behind the Incense Smoke. Community Living, 1.2.

Brandon, D. (1989) Teaching People with Learning Difficulties to Meditate, Self and Society. Spring.

Simply Meditate - a brief introduction to meditation, is available, price £1.50, from David Brandon, Tao, 36 Victoria Parade, Preston PR2 1DT.

Chapter 6

Childhood Recreated

Pat Frankish

My early attempts to do psychotherapy with people with learning difficulties who were emotionally disturbed led me to embrace a theory based
on the work of Mahler, Pine and Bergman (1955). I found I was not working with traditional neuroses but at a more primitive level of personality
development. Mahler's theory of 'psychological birth', which I shall go
on to describe, was relevant to many therapy sessions.

At birth, the relationship between parent and baby is symbiotic. They
are so close as to be almost joined together and both are content so long
as they are not threatened with separation. Much has been written about
bonding, early attachment and its value in personality development. In-
deed, in some cases, where there has been no early attachment figure,
babies have failed to thrive physically as well as psychologically.

Mahler and her colleagues studied babies and mothers over the first
few years of life and identified the first stage of developing independence
as that of *differentiation*. In the first few months of life, the child begins
to recognise that there are different parts of itself and other things that
don't belong. This can be witnessed quite clearly when babies discover
their hands, feet and toys. They begin to take an interest in the environment, people and their own bodies. This is the first sub-phase.

The second sub-phase is called *practising* and ties in closely with vocal
and locomotor development. The early practising phase, overlapping
with differentiation and awareness of the body, coincides with sitting and
crawling, going on to standing and walking. Observation of children indicates that the most important part of the child's world is still the mother
and these other activities could only be 'practised' for short periods in
close proximity to, and regular return to, the mother, whose presence is
taken for granted but not demanded.

During the second year of life, the youngster becomes more and more mobile and in control of the environment. Words are used to make things happen and legs to go away and towards desired objects. As the awareness of separateness grows, there is an increase in separation anxiety. The child notices that the mother is not there or that the distance between them is too great for comfort. This sub-phase is called *rapprochement* and involves a process of testing the relationship - needing closeness, wanting separateness, requiring that mother can accept the ambivalence - for successful resolution. The emotional availability of the mother is paramount. The child returns for emotional refuelling at regular intervals and panics if it is not available. The picture of the toddler exploring and running back to Mum, or playing with regular looks to check that Mum is still there, is very familiar and constitutes a crucial stage of emotional development where the anxiety is maintained at a manageable level and the child is able to internalise and control more and more anxiety.

Assuming that all goes well and rapprochement is navigated successfully, the toddler grows into a separate being with a sense of individuality that will remain and provide the springboard for future emotional stability with a clearly separate personality.

There are many links between this theory and other parts of psychoanalytic thinking, particularly that of Melanie Klein. I use Mahler's theory because behaviours associated with specific sub-phases are clearly defined. It is more straightforward to adapt the theory to my work with people with learning difficulties. They have impaired cognitive functioning, sometimes physical disablement and some disruption of emotional development. During therapy I find that children and adults display the sorts of behaviours described by Mahler, and that they progress towards integrated personality and individuation if I can provide the right sort of security of relatedness for the right stage. It was the rapprochement stage that impressed me first because of the necessary physical and cognitive ability required for the child's control of the situation. Most people with severe handicaps have no words to control their environment and many cannot move to control distances.

Mahler et al describe the effects of difficulties with each sub-phase and the consequent behaviours, the most notable being anxiety symptoms. Some babies and their mothers were extremely uneasy with the symbiotic phase and only began to relax with each other during practising. Others were unable to give up the symbiotic phase and reacted with extreme distress if separation was enforced. Some children walked very early, moved away from their secure base and panicked. The transition through the sub-phases to separation-individuation seemed fraught with danger. However, many seemed successful.

In the case of a child with handicaps, the early symbiotic relationship may be disrupted by hospitalisation or initial rejection. Bonding is a two-way process and an unresponsive child makes it hard for a mother to believe she is needed. The practising sub-phase may be hampered by physical disability or by lack of opportunity. A child with learning difficulties who doesn't cry may spend hours tucked up tidily in a cot, be kept on milk-feeds a long time, and be denied many ordinary experiences. Successful negotiation of the rapprochement sub-phase, if reached at all, is so dependent on cognitive and physical skill as to be unlikely for many youngsters with learning difficulties.

It seemed probable, therefore, that the people referred to me, particularly those with extreme anxiety, had not negotiated the phases. The question was, 'Is it possible to provide a course of therapy that will be a healing experience and allow emotional and personality development to occur?'

....

PETER

Peter was referred when he was 10. He attended the local special school for children with severe learning difficulties. He had no physical handicap but suffered from a speech impediment.

Peter had experienced serious deprivation in early life, not just of the basic requirements such as food and warmth but also of stimulation. He had been confined to a room or a cot for a long time before being taken into local authority care. At the time of referral he was fostered in an excellent home. His Mum was concerned about his anxiety, his rituals and lack of interaction with the family. 'He doesn't seem to have any feelings', she said. The rituals included walking backwards, standing on his head and insisting that the world is upside down, and demanding specific food and drinks. The anxiety included frenzied attempts to climb the walls and panic attacks that looked like cardiac arrest. He rarely smiled and could not accept that anything he was or did was 'good'. Saying 'Good boy!' to him would bring on an anxiety attack and sometimes result in attacks on the perpetrator.

Following Mahler's theory, it appeared that Peter had not experienced the symbiotic sub-phase, or been attached in any healthy way. It is not possible to give up something you've never had. Peter was finding some way of making his world safe. Consequently, he had rituals and obsessions and any interference brought on fear and attack. The first focus of therapy was to establish a therapeutically symbiotic relationship. In natural circumstances, the baby is all powerful, all needs are met and everything is fine. Providing that for a 10-year old boy proved difficult. If I got things wrong, he kicked, bit and spat. But we persevered and from the beginning he seemed to understand our role.

In the early sessions, I had to sit in a particular chair and he sat in my desk chair. He used my dictaphone to talk to me. He would not speak to me directly and I had to repeat what he said to the machine. I also had to get it right! He would go round the room saying, 'eat table', 'eat chair', 'eat flower', and so on.

After several months, he progressed to eating me as well. If I interpreted his words or behaviour, he became angry. I had to accept, that was all. He built bonfires with paper out of the drawer, destroyed tapes, used reels of selotape. He had to take, take, take, but he would never touch my files or work books. In some sessions, I wasn't allowed to speak at all; in others, I could repeat what he said, but say nothing of my own. After some months, he asked for a drink and we went together to fetch it from the kitchen. Later, he wanted a drink and a biscuit (he always took two and no more). We would fetch it, he would eat and drink, then return the glass to the kitchen.

About a year into therapy, Peter began to practise doing other things and allow some two-way intervention. He would walk backwards and insist that I do the same. I said, 'Everything is backwards to you', and he said, 'Yes', and relaxed. He began to use the telephone and the tape recorders; he cut out pictures, often aggressively destroying faces, searched frantically through magazines for floors and ceilings. It seemed very important that he could call things by the names he chose and that nothing bad should happen. He experimented with everything in the room and became fascinated by a squeaky toy. It was the wrong colour and he insisted that I get a white one next time. This seemed to be a test of whether I really could provide what he needed, so I got the toy. This sort of omnipotence is described by Melanie Klein and belongs to the very early stages of psychic life, where the baby is in total control and anything thwarting is felt as persecution. Whichever theory I adhered to, I had to survive the process without spoiling it, allow Peter to experience himself as being in control but safe from attack.

Gradually, there was a change. He began to be less concerned about the order of events, and arrived for therapy with enthusiasm, running to my room. I still had to sit in the same chair but I was included in activities. I could even hold the tape recorder, which meant him coming very close. He began to dislike the end of sessions and became very anxious when I said it was nearly time to go.

Six months later, he's beginning to smile, to look at me properly and interact. I am allowed to talk and interpret, to explain about his early life and the effect on him, to help him see that the foster home is different. He acknowledges that he loves his Mum but can't bear to be too close. There's a great deal of trial and error on my part because of his speech problem but there's no doubt when I'm wrong. 'Shut up', says Peter, and ignores me, sometimes for the rest of the time. Another feature that appeared when the rapprochement period was well under way was visiting the toilet. Again, using different theories, we could say that he's passed from the oral to the anal or sexual stage; we could speculate on castration anxiety if he was perceiving me as a powerful woman. But it seemed more about checking that I would still be there when he came back and that I could trust him to go. If I'd showed anxiety, he might have felt insecure and returned to the 'nest'. It felt as though we were working together. I was also questioning the extent of his learning difficulties and the role that imperfect personality formation had on his level of functioning. This was evidenced by the sudden acquisition of telling the time. He used this to control both his anxiety about the ending itself by telling me that it was time to go and putting his coat on and going. The ambivalence towards me was there in everything he did. Could I tolerate it? I knew that if I wanted to test the usefulness of the theory, I had to tolerate it and wait, keep the sessions regular, keep my behaviour and availability constant.

Peter still has rituals. He still returns to some of the more extreme ones at times of stress. But they are over very quickly and we haven't seen a panic attack for months. He smiles; he looks whole; he's growing up.

It is relatively easy to think of this sort of treatment as being suitable for children. The next question I asked myself was, 'Can it work for adults? Is it appropriate?' The problem seemed two-fold: how seriously disturbed an adult who had an incomplete personality might be, and whether it was possible to provide a therapeutic milieu in which to encourage further growth. The people who have the problem are likely to be displaying quite difficult and inappropriate behaviour because of their anxiety. People with handicaps who behave in an anti-social way have a hard life. It seemed worth trying.

DEBBIE

Debbie was resident in a long-stay hospital when I first knew her. She was 24 and had been in hospital since she was 17. She was refusing to eat or co-operate, becoming abusive and aggressive when attempts were made to coerce her. One of 20 on an understaffed ward, she was causing concern. She was on anti-psychotic medication and night time medication, but slept little, ate nothing and looked wild-eyed. There was a search for a 'cause' and various possibilities were proposed, among them trauma during a visit home, anger at a new admission, change of staff and pre-menstrual tension. When I met her she looked frightened but agreed to go to my room. During the first session, she sat and cried the whole time but agreed to come again the next week.

Debbie came from a large family and Mum struggled to cope with her excitable and uncontrolled behaviour. She had been excluded from a number of schools and the adult training centre; hence her admission to hospital. She loved her Mum and wanted to be with her, frequently talking to herself as though she was her mother. I speculated on the possibility of them being unable to move on from the symbiotic phase.

I visited Mum to see if there was a chance she could do the work with her daughter with my support. It was clear that would not be possible so I decided to try therapy. The first part would involve the transference of the symbiotic relationship from Mum to me.

Debbie had severe learning difficulties and much of her speech was echolalic (ie. she repeated what was said to her). Many of her mannerisms and reactions were those of a very young child, but others were more age-appropriate. A doll she owned appeared to be a transitional object (an object which takes on some of the powers of the secure person and bridges the gap between symbiotic attachment and separation (Winnicott, 1971)) but there were many objections to her having it and it was usually kept in her locker.

The early sessions were very fraught. She screamed and cried, talked to herself, accused people of hurting her, went through her full repertoire of nursery rhymes and songs, expecting nothing from me except my presence and tolerance. These I gave for an hour at a time and we continued on a weekly basis. It wasn't long before she was greeting me like a long lost mother and valuing the time we spent together.

So far so good. The attachment process was successful. I had been advised not to take on people who had extreme dependency and attachment needs for psychotherapy. I began to wonder at my wisdom but as Debbie was now attached and working I had to continue.

I remembered that the practising sub-phase involved discovering things about yourself, others and the environment, so I introduced some task-centred work to the sessions. These involved basic things, like pens, paper and toys. Debbie began to write, in her way, letters to people she knew. She didn't write to me which seemed an acknowledgement that we didn't communicate in that formal way. While writing, she would talk about events and people and respond to my interpretation of what she was saying. We began to build up a picture, or a story, of her life so far. It was very clear in her mind and I was corrected if I got facts wrong from previous weeks. We also did some basic relaxation together which she began to use when she became anxious in sessions. She would say, 'We'll do some deep breathing now', and stop the conversation, thereby keeping control and not addressing issues that were too painful.

A noticeable feature during sessions was that Debbie never used bad language, although this was one of the complaints about her behaviour. It was almost as though swearing belonged to something, somewhere and someone else.

A year into therapy I decided to risk the wrath of the authorities and provide a doll. It was added to the collection of other things. I was thinking particularly of the rapprochement sub-phase and transitional objects. I needed to find out if Debbie could use a thing, rather than a person, to feel safe and if she could detach herself from me in a healthier way than she had from Mum.

There was always a lot of physical contact between us during therapy. Debbie would frequently cry on my lap, play 'round and round the garden' and other contact games. I hoped this would be transferred to the doll, with me there if needed, so she could function without the need for a symbiotic attachment. It seemed to work. She took to the doll immediately and, after a time, began to treat it as a person (herself, I think), talking to it, playing games with it, all the time checking I was there and didn't disapprove. She never asked if she could take it away but replaced it in the drawer at the end of the session, with the certainty that she would be back and the doll would be there.

The symptoms with which Debbie was first referred disappeared within weeks and eating problems have not returned. The noisy and disruptive behaviour still occurs but less frequently and she has moved into a community project. This has meant she sees me in a different place. On

the first occasion I forgot to take the doll. This was a real test of her abilty 'to stand alone', at least in therapy sessions. There had been a few occasions where she had been quite detached from me but the doll had always been there.

I needed to know if she would manage - and she did. She wanted to know where the doll was and when reassured it was still in the drawer she understood and showed no anxiety. We talked about ordinary things, her new life and the future.

Debbie has not cried or screamed for months. The last time was after an incident which upset her. She was able to express her feelings in the session and felt better. She is not 'together' and individuated all the time, however, and still talks to herself and has occasional outbursts of swearing and shouting. Hopefully, her periods of control will extend and the incidents decrease as she has more experience of being separate without anxiety.

....

The two case studies suggest that it is more difficult to apply Mahler's theory to adults but that it is nevertheless useful. They suggest that therapy needs to be longer for adults. The two people had very different life experiences: Debbie, although able to be herself, experienced something bad that would make most people angry and defensive. The results are sufficiently promising for me to continue.

This approach, and its therapeutic effect, provokes other questions. One is about early schooling but that debate belongs elsewhere. Another more relevant question concerns that of therapeutic environments. There are insufficient therapists to provide individual therapy for people like Debbie and Peter. Perhaps it is possible to provide living environments that can meet their needs, if we can identify those at a given time. The approach's dual themes are dependence and security. It is possible they could be achieved by attachment to a place or a group, provided they are seen as benevolent, rather than to an individual. Because Mahler's theory is relatively straightforward, we can work out what stage someone is at in their emotional development from their behaviour. The person described as 'attention-seeking' seems to me to be either seeking a symbiotic closeness or is in the rapprochement crisis. The difference can be identified by the degree of anxiety and 'drive' they demonstrate. The person who panics and becomes disruptive when left alone is still not able to believe in their own existence when others are not there. There is a need for symbiotic dependence which should be provided. Adults whose personality development is as fragile as this would gain more from attaching to a place. Their needs are too great to be met by staff and staff rotas. Following the theory makes it possible to devise a plan to give the basic security needed to facilitate personality development. It is not as effective as individual therapy but it helps.

In the past, institutions provided the 'safe place' and many people became very dependent on them and unwilling to move. This has produced a tendency for clinicians and administrators to advise against the development of dependence, or over-dependence. Staff are generally advised not to become too involved with the people they care for and clinging behaviour is discouraged. It would seem institutions have as stultifying an effect on the emotional maturity of people with learning difficulties as their families of origin. Disruption of the symbiotic relationship with the primary carer may have resulted in challenging behaviour and hospitalisation. The young person cannot move on emotionally until that primary need is met. The institution could meet it but the fear of dependence developing militates against providing a really therapeutic 'holding' environment. Thus, many years later, the person is still desperately trying to find someone or something reliable and strong enough to hold him. If he has felt safer in the institution than anywhere else, he will resist leaving and exhibit behaviour similar to that of early childhood, thus ensuring he is returned to base.

To provide real healing, it is necessary to examine both the effectiveness of the 'holding' and the ways in which people can progress if they are 'held'. Mahler's theory could be used to clarify the needs of the individual on the basis of what is said through behaviour. From this base line, experiences and environments can be planned that will encourage progress along the road to psychological birth and peace of mind.

References
Mahler, M.S. Pine, F. & Bergman, A. (1955). Psychological Birth of the Human Infant. Hutchinson.
Winnicott, D. (1971) Playing and Reality. Tavistock.

Chapter 7

Unconscious Imagery

Alison Buckley

Although the term 'art therapy' has been in use since the 1940s, and training courses have been run since the 1970s, art therapy has only been established as a therapeutic discipline with a recognised training since 1981. There are now three courses offering DHSS approved postgraduate training for art therapists. It combines clinical and theoretical studies, experiential workshops, the development of self-awareness and the therapist's own creativity. There are approximately 400 registered art therapists in the UK the majority of whom work in London and the South East. There are few art therapists in Scotland, the North of England and Wales. They are usually employed as members of a multi-disciplinary treatment team working with a variety of client groups in settings such as psychiatric hospitals, day centres, prisons, special schools and institutions for the care of people with learning difficulties.

Perhaps because it is a relatively new profession, the aims and objectives of art therapy are not widely known. Although it is generally accepted by others in the 'caring' professions that most art activity has therapeutic qualities, there are some common misconceptions about what it is.

It is not a form of art teaching. The client is not required to be good at art and the therapist does not aim to impart art skills. The emphasis is on self-expression by the client, using spontaneous painting, free from preconceived ideas.

It does not provide a key to understanding pictures in a universal way, in the manner of a newspaper horoscope.

It is not an activity designed to offer distraction from inner conflicts but one which might directly assist the client towards a better understanding of his difficulties.

It is not a substitute for general art activities in hospitals, day centres and other institutions.

Art therapy has borrowed heavily from the theories and concepts of psycho-analysis. The key concept common to probably all art therapy, and which further distinguishes it from art teaching, is the acknowledgement of the unconscious: 'the idea that there exists mental activity of which the subject is unaware but which none the less exerts a dynamic effect on his behaviour' (Rycroft, 1968). Evidence comes from dreaming as well as from the way in which we find ourselves repeating unsatisfactory life experiences or relationships.

Art therapists believe that spontaneous painting expresses the unconscious. Depending on his own theoretical framework and technique and on the client, the art therapist may help the client to make conscious the underlying content of his imagery by encouraging him to express his associations to it.

The art activity and art product provide a means of communication between the client and the therapist in addition to verbal and non- verbal processes. This suggests that art therapy can be especially valuable for clients with learning difficulties whose use of speech or understanding of words is limited. Like everyone else, these people have a range of conscious and unconscious emotions but may need greater help not only to understand their feelings but initially to express them.

I am often impressed by the richness of feelings and phantasy which people with learnings difficulties are able to express in the context of the relationship between therapist and client.

....

MARGARET

Margaret is a 48-year old woman who has been in residential care in one place since her mid-teens. During her early years, she lived with her parents. She has been diagnosed as having severe and widespread organic brain damage of unknown cause. She has a long history of grand mal epilepsy and aggressive behaviour. She can be sensitive and irritable but, just as characteristically, sociable and affectionate. Both parents are alive and maintain contact with her.

I first worked with Margaret in an 'open' art group (1). Margaret

(1) An 'open' group is one in which clients are free to work as they choose, independently of each other. The therapist's role is supportive rather than directive. Any discussion of the art work tends to be between the individual client and the therapist rather than the group as a whole. The therapist modifies his responses because of the presence of other clients.

would try to monopolise my attention by talking to me almost continually at the expense of the other clients. Her difficulty in recalling verbal information made listening to her a strain. Increasingly, she raised topics which could not be discussed satisfactorily in that setting. I felt I could help her more in a weekly individual session.

I explained the reasons for offering a 'private' time and that it would be for 50 minutes each week, at the same place, on the same day. The constancy of time, place and therapist, along with the notion of having uninterrupted 'private' time, are enormously important. From the start of the work these factors convey to the client a sense of worth and respect and, given the constraints of institutional life, may become even more valued.

I collect Margaret from her 'training group'. Ideally, the client, would be brought by someone else, if unable to attend independently, as fetching encourages phantasies of the therapist's needs rather than the client's need for something the therapist has. It also, from the start, makes the client feel like a child.

However, such requirements cannot always be easily met and compromise is necessary. In the short walk to the art therapy room, I try not to be drawn into conversation so we both feel the work is contained in the therapy room. For the same reason, I try to limit any contact I have with Margaret around the institution. Once inside the room, we usually talk for a time and then Margaret does some art work. She enjoys painting and will invariably choose to paint rather than draw.

Margaret paints carefully and deliberately, with great concentration. She does not relate to her paintings on a symbolic level. As with much observed behaviour, my ideas about what her art work might mean for her are inferred. Her paintings are repetitive with little variation between them indicating a constant working over of the same thoughts without change or progress.

Working from the outer edges of the paper, Margaret paints thick borders, one inside another, filling up the paper as she works towards the centre. The borders suggest a need for containment, a framework. They form a pattern which is predictable and safe. She leaves no spaces that imagination might fill. Her paintings seem controlled and show little spontaneity. The issue of control may relate to Margaret's epilepsy. During a grand mal fit she loses control and may fear being overwhelmed.

In common with many institutionalised patients with whom I work, Margaret expresses no desire to take her creations away with her or any particular interest in what becomes of them. This may originate from a conviction that their thoughts and products are not worth keeping. I aim to convey a sense of ownership and value in their work by telling clients it is kept in a named folder.

A dominant theme with Margaret is her wish to get married and have a baby. In our early sessions, Margaret would ask me if I was married. I try to avoid giving answers to such questions as this limits the possiblity of understanding better what else they might mean. The relief that a 'favourable' answer might bring is temporary and one less favourably received would reinforce her envy. Without help, Margaret returns to the same question, often within minutes, suggesting that the underlying meaning, and the experience of differences between us, continue to be a source of phantasy and curiosity with which she has difficulties.

Margaret focuses her talk about marriage on the wedding. She talks of the conventions of a wedding, with all the appearances of normality. 'My Dad's going to give me away'. This may be significant. Her father 'gave her away' once before, into the care of professionals. She may express an unconscious hope that he will give her away to a man who needs her more than he is felt to have done.

Margaret's phantasy lover is spoken of as if real. Her powerful phantasies indicate a sexual content and a desire for exploration. She tells me he says, 'You're my darling. I want to take you in my arms.' She wants to be someone's darling, to be special to someone and also, perhaps, to feel really held and contained.

In our sessions Margaret does not link her desire for a wedding with her wish to have a baby. She tells me her parents want her to have a baby. This may be a projection of her own wish, partly perhaps to compensate them but also to prove she's not handicapped. 'It would make me better,' she said.

Margaret's deeply felt ideas about her mother's disappointment in her own handicapped baby resonate in her relationships with primary carers (therapist, nurses, keyworker). She convinced herself that her keyworker, Jane, was leaving to have a baby. Margaret had been Jane's 'baby' in their teacher/pupil (adult/child) relationship. She may have felt that only a more loved baby could cause Jane to leave.

In our recent meetings Margaret has often spoken of her epileptic fits and of her wish for them to stop. I imagine she wishes this not only because of the unpleasantness of the fits but because they may be reminders of the handicapped parts of herself. Some discussion of her fits feature in the following account of an art therapy session. I fetched Margaret from her 'training' group for her session. Before we left her group room, she said: 'I'm not married yet.' There was an urgency in her need to talk. In the context of our marriage (the therapy relationship) this may have been a way of saying she has felt on her own since we last met. In our previous meeting, Margaret had talked about getting engaged and asked if I would get an engagement ring. I felt she was asking me to enter her phantasy world.

In the art therapy room the same urgency to speak was apparent. She began talking before taking her coat off, and continued without showing interest in art activities. She spoke about a fellow resident going on holiday to the Holy Land. She said: 'I told him all about it for when he goes there.' Margaret comes from a religious family and holds firm but simplistic Christian ideas. From experience of Margaret's ideas I wonder now whether the omnipotence suggested by her remark concealed envy of someone getting 'closer' to God. Perhaps also contained in her comment is some idea of her fellow resident going to the place where miracles occurred and might still occur. This may explain the apparent jump in her subject matter as she told of the 'miracles' she hopes the nursing staff will work.

Margaret: *Nurse Thompson is trying to get my heart better because of my fits.*

The reference to her heart may relate to an idea that if she did not have fits she might be able to receive the love she wants; she might be more lovable.

Margaret: *Well, Frank* (a nursing assistant) *is trying to stop my fits.*

Me: *You'd like your fits to stop.*

Margaret: *Yes.* (Pause). *Nurse Thompson and Frank are taking me on holiday with them.*

Margaret introduced another theme, implying that the staff (a male/female couple) were planning to take her on holiday 'with them' as if on their own 'private, family holiday.

I suggested that she'd like to have no fits on holiday. I reminded her she proudly told me last year that she'd had no fits on holiday but the 'baby' (a multiply handicapped resident) had. The term 'baby' has sometimes been used by Margaret in our work as an expression of contempt. The way in which she uses the word suggests contempt of the baby part of herself.

Me: *So you think only babies have fits...*

Margaret: *Yes.*

Me: *And having fits makes you feel like a baby...*

Margaret: *Yes.*

Margaret began to talk about when her fits started.

Margaret: *I started them... my mother started them... when I went to Trafford House* (a special school).

Margaret seemed to think someone had caused her fits to start and linked this to being moved from her parents' home. Her confusion over who was to blame suggests she may have a number of ideas. It would be of little use to offer explanations of organic factors without helping her to understand what the explanations she has chosen might mean for her and what purpose they serve.

As Margaret was already having fits when she left her parents' home she may have felt that being epileptic and brain-damaged meant that she was not good enough or lovable enough for her parents to want her. I questioned another idea, pointing out that she had said her mother started the fits. I suggested she felt her parents caused the fits to start by sending her away. Margaret agreed. I tried to put into words for her how that might have felt. She became quiet and solemn.

After a while, she got up and moved to the opposite table (away from me but still facing me). I felt she was distancing herself from difficult feelings. She began to draw, using materials already on the table. By using these she avoided asking for anything. She may feel that when she moves away, or is moved away, she must find ways of managing with her own resources.

She drew a border with a felt pen, inside which she drew part of a second and third border. She worked faster than usual, determinedly, perhaps with some aggression, concentrating on her work and pressing hard with the pen. I reminded her that we had five minutes left. She hurried to finish her drawing, filling in the middle more loosely. Whilst doing this she asked, 'When will I see you again?' I told her we would meet next Tuesday as usual. After a pause, she checked, 'Next Tuesday?'

It seemed hard for Margaret to leave at the end of the session. She dawdled, complaining a number of times that it was cold outside. I said

Margaret's drawing

The group painting

81

that she feels put out in the cold when the session ends. Our work keeps her mind warm, but outside, where she has to manage on her own, things get frozen and fixed. She started to look through a magazine found near the door. She was delaying leaving and did not respond when I reminded her that our session had ended. I felt she was hoping I would offer a magazine to take away, something concrete of mine to bridge the gap between this session and the next.

I acknowledged how hard she felt it was to leave and emphasised that we would meet again in a weeks time. 'Next Tuesday', she repeated, 'All right.' She smiled warmly and left the room.

ART THERAPY GROUP

My second clinical illustration is taken from a 'closed' group which I run jointly with another art therapist from an adult training centre. This group offered members an experience different to the 'open' groups with which they were familiar. We felt a formal group could encourage them to relate more to each other and to take and share responsibility, at least within the group setting. We hoped they could express feelings and experience mutual support.

There are a number of rules and expectations. The sessions are private and have a fixed time (90 minutes), place and membership. There is an expectation that the group members (but not the leaders) will paint together on one large, vertical piece of paper, and that the group will sit together around the painting (2) to discuss it.

In selecting group members we had two main criteria: that they would be able to cope with the anxiety of this unfamiliar way of working and that they could benefit from the group experience.

There are five people in the group: Janet, Pat and Maureen from the ATC, and Barry and John from the residential setting where the session takes place.

This account is from the ninth meeting. Maureen was absent because of illness. The session illustrates some features common to the early stages in the life of therapy groups. The members are familiar with the pattern of the sessions. They have overcome some of the anxiety caused by not knowing what might be expected. However, they are still functioning quite separately in the group with little sense of unity.

The talking takes the form of separate monologues rather than group

---

(2) The term painting is used here to mean all forms of picture-making.

discussion. This is reflected in the painting where each person is working in his own space and on his own 'picture'.

It can be useful to consider each member's behaviour in terms of serving a group function. For example, Janet talks at every opportunity, making it difficult for anyone else to speak. She unintentionally demonstrates how painful sharing is. Other members may allow her to take on this function for them.

The session began as usual with some time for talking together. The group agreed to have half an hour for painting.

John, a small balding middle-aged man who finds it particularly hard to be in the group, moved between the group painting and his own clerical paper folding. He slapped on paint like a decorator, using a decorator's brush and a good deal of posturing. His behaviour typically mimics male staff. He appeared to carelessly cover part of Barry's painting.

Barry, a stocky man in his late twenties with cropped black hair, worked slowly but deliberately, in silence. He had started painting before John moved into the small space beside him. Barry painted a house, an image he often uses. Although the house looks quite bold towards the top, it has no base and appears unrooted and unstable. Barry had finished and was sitting down when he noticed John painting over his work. I observed a flicker of what looked like panic on Barry's face before it was quickly concealed.

Janet, a plumpish young woman with red hair, took up a large central area for her painting of a T-shirt which her mother had ordered for her. She painted over and over the image as she repeated the story behind it, complaining that the T-shirt had not arrived and blaming her mother. Her persistent complaint seemed about more than just missing a T-shirt. Janet feels that her mother never 'comes up with the goods' and she has to rely on her own inadequate resources. As the outfit took shape on the paper, she sounded pleased with her work and painted the words, 'Ha, so there'. Janet often uses the group painting to 'write letters' as if, fearing that she won't be heard, she has to spell out her words.

Pat, a neat, bespectacled middle-aged woman, worked silently, well away from the others, intent on drawing a family and two houses. The children in Pat's drawing are represented by a less developed style than the adults. The father is drawn, as she always represents men, with a two-part body as if he might have something extra below. Like Janet, Pat reinforces her lines by working over them.

The paper on which the group paint is mounted vertically so that it has a clear top and a bottom, thus allowing the group the possibility of one image. When it was time to stop painting, the group sat together in front of their work.

John: *I painted that.*

I asked if he wanted to say more.

John: *Yeah. I did that.*

John was embarrassed by the attention. Smiling, he rocked in his chair and muttered about things outside the session. It was progress for him to join the discussion; he had previously sat apart.

I turned the attention back to the painting by noting that John's work had encroached on Barry's. When asked what he thought about this, Barry replied, 'Nothing.' I suggested it might feel easier to think nothing than to think about the something that had intruded upon his painting. I recalled an occasion when Barry had obliterated Pat's picture with his own. I reminded him that we had discussed how that felt.

Me: *I wonder how you felt when John painted over your work.*

Barry: (after a slight pause): *Awful.*

My immediate response was pleasure that he had expressed feelings, but I was surprised by his unusual directness. I wondered whether it might have been partly a deliberate response to give us what he felt we wanted.

Me: *Perhaps you were surprised when you saw it and thought, 'Hey! He can't do that. That's my painting'.*

John: *That's not very nice at all* (spoken as if to himself).

John got up, went to the sink and washed his hands (literally, washing his hands of the 'dirty' business). Janet took the opportunity to ask, 'Do you know about my painting?'

Sarah, my co-therapist, reassured Janet that her turn would come.

I tried to help John rejoin the group by suggesting that he had needed to get up because of the discomfort. I asked if he felt able to join us again. He returned, saying, 'I did this', with a mixture of pride and confession. Sarah asked Barry if he wanted to say more about his painting and feelings. He did not answer. He looked around the group and smiled, keeping us all in suspense. I remarked that he was smiling, at which he rubbed his hands together gleefully as if he enjoying, at that moment, the power

84

of withheld speech. Sarah asked again if he wanted to say anything else. Barry remained silent.

Janet: (in a patronising voice): *Well, Barry?*

Janet feels that Barry is less able than her.

Barry: *Hello, Barry* (patronising her in return).

Janet: *What about your painting?*

Barry did not answer but continued to smile.
Sarah asked if someone else would like to talk about their work. Janet jumped at the chance.

Janet: *It's a skirt and top, tennis skirt and top.*

Sarah: *What else is there?*

Janet: *A handbag, an Alice-band, a hat and shoes... what my Mum's going to get for me. That's my Mum* (indicating a crude, black stick figure on the painting).

Me: *Can you read for us what you've written?*

Janet: *Well, it's..* (she hesitates, unable to read what she has written) *..I put T-shirt, I put T-shirt up there. £1.50, see. It's a mauve T-shirt with stripes. It says, 'T-shirt'.*

Sarah: *And what's that?*

Janet: *That's if Dan* (her boyfriend) *gets me a T-shirt then I won't have to ask me Mum to get it.*

Me: *It reads, 'Dan will buy it for me'.*

Janet: *Yeah. He will buy it for me.* (Her voice became croaky).

Me: *You sound upset about that.*

Janet: *I just do.*

We learnt that Janet feels she asks for little but still her mother and boyfriend don't give her what she wants. She has to rely on herself.

Me: *You feel your Mum doesn't give you what you want...*

Janet: *That's right, that's right.*

Me: *...and Dan doesn't seem to give you what you want.*

Janet: *Seems like it, yeah, does seem like it. I've got to do everything for meself... get me own stuff.*

Sarah: *You feel you've got to get your own help and your own love.*

Janet: Y*eah!* (strong, angry, affirmative voice) *Could be right, couldn't it?*

With only ten minutes left, Sarah asked Pat if she would like an opportunity to speak. Pat, who had been silent throughout, spoke immediately but hesitantly about her drawing.

Pat: *...the... the houses, and then that's the grass and the... the people.*

Sarah: *Can you tell us a bit about the people, who they are?*

Pat: *Just any people.*

Pat's answers to our questions about her drawing were brief and non-committal. She often followed her answers with 'That's all'. She was not willing to talk but rather needing us to prompt.

The figures were a family, a man (with the two-part body), a woman (on the left, with pink hair) and three little girls. Pat told us the mother lived in one house and the father in the other. She was unclear about where the children lived. Pat talked more freely, telling us about her own family and the many homes she's lived in, including one 'with the handicapped people'. She seemed confused over how many brothers and sisters she has but told us she never sees her sisters. This suggests links with the girls in her picture for whom she does not have an image of a home.

Pat offered a lot of tantalising material in the last minutes of the session. This is a common feature of therapy groups and it is worth considering why members, perhaps unconsciously, choose this time to talk about things which cannot be followed up in the session. The painting is useful here as it provides a record of the session which can be referred back to. It also provides the group leaders, and the group, with a concrete means of reviewing progress.

....

Fundamental to the theory and practice of art therapy is the belief that most people, including those with learning difficulties, have 'a latent capacity to project... inner conflicts into visual form' (Naumberg, 1958). The case illustrations support this belief and demonstrate the value to the client of a private time when they can feel heard and understood.

References
Naumberg, M (1958) Art Therapy: its Scope and Function. In Hammer, E.F. (ed) Clinical Applications of Projective Drawings. Springfield, Ill., C.C. Thomas.
Rycroft,C (1986) A Critical Dictionary of Psychoanalysis. Harmondsworth, Penguin.

Further reading
Dalley, T (ed) (1984) Art as Therapy. Tavistock.
Dalley, T. et al (1987) Images of Art Therapy. Tavistock.

Acknowledgements
I wish to record my appreciation to Valerie Sinason of the Tavistock Clinic, London, for her enthusiasm and encouragement in the writing of this chapter and in her supervision of my work. I am also grateful to Anthony Cantle with whom I discussed my ideas for this chapter and who made many helpful comments.

Further information can be obtained from the British Association of Art Therapists, 11A Richmond Road, Brighton BN2 3RL.

Chapter 8

Professional Behaviours

David Brandon

People who have a mixture of 'mental handicap' and 'mental illness' labels raise extremely complex issues for our existing services. The empires of mental illness and mental handicaps and their respective professionalised training have a very separate recent history. One has remained relatively medicalised whilst the other has become much more psychological, based on learning perspectives rather than those of sickness. To cover these fundamental differences and our confusion, we have tended to develop strange phrases like 'challenging behaviours'. It is our own behaviour we need to challenge.

Current practices in working with people with learning difficulties and so called 'behaviour disorders' have tended to be predominantly controlling and even sometimes punishment based. Essentially, they reflect the needs of systems rather than persons. No one should be surprised that in an age dominated by technology, the silicon chip and massive exploitation of the planet's resources, we should develop ways of dealing with severely disabled people founded in white coated human technology, using intrusive and controlling strategies directed at managing cases rather than ordinary human healing.

Punishment of severely disabled people is widespread and effectively masked by concepts of 'treatment', intrusive programmes cloaked in healing mythologies. The use of amonia sprays, time-out regimes and restrictive straps are common, particularly in the United States (McGee et al, 1987). Such systems are founded on authoritarian values and are fundamentally undemocratic, denying the essential citizenship of the person with handicaps. 'I am here to teach you the rules (mine and the systems which pay me) whether you like it or not and it will be for your own good.' Such approaches are based on coldness and social distance, seeing the other person as somehow negatively different from ourselves.

In the 1950s, the late Canadian psychiatrist, the eminent Dr Ewen Cameron, then President of the World Psychiatric Association, believed that mental illness was caused by memories and brain patterns which were hard to shift. In Montreal, he prepared patients for treatment by giving them drugs which induced sleep lasting for ten days. Still asleep the patient was given up to 60 shock treatments over a period of 30 days. By then the patient was in a dependent, child-like state. Other patients were deprived of sensory experiences by leaving them in a dark silent room for up to 16 days (Thomas, 1988).

In the early 1980s, I found patients in Cheshire mental handicap units bound by arms and legs to chairs and beds, often for several hours in the day. It was claimed to be part of their behaviour modification programme. Chronic neglect, leaving patients in the same seat at the same table all day long, the only interruption being large spoonfulls of cold and tasteless food, was common.

Examine this quote. 'No one should apply punishment as a treatment procedure without full awareness, exploration and discussion of its ethical implications and never before less drastic measures have been considered....no one should undertake to punish self-injurious behaviour who is not prepared to invest much time and effort in establishing adaptive response patterns that can take the place of the suppressed behaviour and serve the child as a means of obtaining social re-inforcers....' (Ross, 1981). This extract is used with approval in a recent standard mental handicap textbook, which adds, 'In part, this means that punishment techniques are rarely, if ever, justified unless strenuous efforts are in hand to implement a positive, carefully monitored training programme.' (Yule and Carr, 1988). The significant word is 'unless', used to justify intrusive strategies as a last resort. Is there any real justification for that?

It may seem surprising that counselling and psychotherapy, seemingly such inherently gentle approaches, can also be both intrusive and extremely coercive. Ideas and relationships can bind and manipulate even more efficaciously than drugs and leather restraints. At the heart of these approaches is a really intense relationship, which has amongst its ingredients - transferrence. People usually let counsellors in really close, past most of their defences. We are in a position to be more subtly intrusive than others. Therapists can easily misuse their powers through the force of personality and a misguided and dogmatic evangelism. We have to examine intent and result as well as method and technique. Much counselling hides substantial inequalities in power.

The late Don Bannister wrote 'Clearly, the relationship between therapist and client is initially neither reciprocal nor equal. If you are the therapist then you and the client sit on either side of your desk, in your office, on your patch. Your presence signifies qualifications, expertise and prestige; the client's presence signifies that he or she has 'given in', 'confessed failure'. You, as therapist, represent (socially, if not in fact) the healthy ordered life while the client represents 'sickness' and confusion.'(1983).

David Boadella (1980) describes scenes from therapeutic groups in which participants have been tyrannised, humiliated and beaten up. Working in the encounter group movement in the early seventies, I saw people injured, particularly broken ankles and ricked backs, from aggressive fighting, with few boundaries established in such groups.

Peter Lomas (1987) comments, 'It seems likely that people will disclose themselves most fully when they are in an environment in which they feel free to do so; that is, when they feel that they will not be condemned, ridiculed, exploited or punished, and when the evidence necessary to enable them to make a sound judgement is accessible to them.....The therapist who coerces is not searching for the truth: she believes she has the truth and intends to force it upon the recipient by means that themselves may not be truthful.' That is an incipient danger in all forms of therapeutic processes which is why it is wise for counsellors to be continually supervised in practice. That is one way of placing some boundaries on spreading megalomania.

Nikolas Rose (1986) makes a much more profound criticism of the psychotherapeutic process - about the professional annexation of ordinary human experiences. 'These therapies of normality transpose the difficulties inherent in living on to a psychological register; they become not intractable features of desire and frustration but malfunctions of the psychological apparatus that are remediable through the operation of particular techniques. The self is thus opened up, a new continent for exploitation by the entrepreneurs of the psyche, who both offer us an image of a life of maximised intellectual, commercial, sexual or personal fulfilment and assure us that we can achieve it with the assistance of the technicians of subjectivity.' Through the development of the therapies a whole host of these mind hucksters selling their dangerous wares, develop an expanding service industry. We take away the ordinary stuff of human love and affection with the increasing aridity of modern neighbourhoods and replace it with people paid to smile at others -   social workers rather

91

than friends and neighbours. Neighbours have become something you watch on TV.

John O'Brien (1988) rejects completely the use of pain and punishment in working with people with severe disabilities. 'People who wish to build up positive relationships and less violent social settings will follow two simple rules: if in doubt, do not cause pain; and, act positively to create conditions that decrease the occurrence of pain. Right living lies in the long term struggle to apply those two rules in the creation of fitting responses to the difficult situations arising from engagement with people with severe disabilities who injure themselves or others.'

'Behaviourally challenging' persons have often experienced 'treatment' processes that totally ignore their physical and emotional well-being, whilst denying the context of their behaviour. Institutions are de-humanising not only for the patients but also for the staff who work there. Jean Lally (1988) points to an often overlooked cause of anger: 'Frequent anger may be a cry for help, a sign that something is deeply wrong which cannot be expressed or remedied. To help a person in this situation to lead a happy and socially integrated life, the causes of the anger must be determined and means of reducing them considered.'

At the outset, we have to ask what the challenging behaviour is about. It is different in quality and nature to describe someone as 'behaviourially disturbed' or 'presenting with verbal aggression' than saying they are 'angry'. For the first two we reach for the tranquilliser bottle or behaviour programme: for the last, we ask why they are angry. It is difficult to penetrate professionalised labels because they traditionally conceal so many problems and contain service-centred perspectives. They may conceal our own anger as well as that of the person they describe. Who is being behaviourially challenged? How does it feel to be left alone in a time-out room ? How does it feel to be allowed repeatedly to hit yourself in the face? If we are to experience our presence as valued by others that must mean feeling safe and emotionally secure.

The emergence of disruptive or destructive behaviours is often the person's only way of fighting back at a seemingly hostile world which is controlling, coercive, incomprehensible and non-responsive. Attempts to communicate their frustration are rarely encouraged as David Anderson has noted: 'Mentally handicapped people are often robbed of their speech because other people do not believe they have ideas or that any ideas they might have would be of value; they do not allow time for halting or diffident expression, or are frightened of what the handicapped people might say' (1982).

We are beginning to develop and to receive a wide variety of different processes for assisting the development of people with learning difficulties. Feurstein, an Israeli psychologist working in the field of learning difficulties for more than thirty years, has developed a dynamic notion of intellectual potential as opposed to the more static notions which are currently popular. 'Instrumental' or 'conceptual enrichment' as it is variously known offers extremely systematic training to develop intelligence. Feurstein (Sharron, 1987) maintains that instrumental enrichment is a way of 'smuggling in a theory of child development and under- development'.

Just as revolutionary is the system of gentle teaching, developed in Nebraska, USA. This challenges paid staff to question their practices and to develop new values, moving towards mutually humanising and liberating teaching approaches. It is essential to model and teach the person that there is value and goodness inherent in human relationships. Teaching the value and goodness of human presence and participation leads to bonding rather than bondage. Punishment systems lead to submission and domination as well as the demeaning of the punisher, whilst bonding encourages mutual liberation. A posture of solidarity, becoming at one with the other, encourages closeness, warmth, acceptance and tolerance.

At the heart of social interactions lies equity. At the start of relationships with people who have severe learning difficulties, giving and receiving are necessarily imbalanced. We will give much and receive little - creating participation when it is not wanted and giving reward when it is not appreciated. Ancient, savage feelings may bubble up from our being. As greater bonding takes place, that inequity lessens if allowed and teaching strategies which move us away from mutual human liberation avoided.

Our central purpose is reward teaching - both as an end and a means. It completely eliminates the need for persons to hurt themselves or others. Distancing is replaced by interdependence; compliance is replaced by reciprocity and respect; independence replaced by interdependence. A pivotal component is redirection. It consists of teaching responses that refocus the interactional flow from undesirable to rewarding interactions.

Gentle teaching approaches involve a constant review of our goals, creative teaching skills and persevering effort. It is crucial to create opportunities to give reward. If that only involves ignoring maladaptive behaviours, it will not work. Reward giving and eventually reward sharing comprise the core of our actions.

Our encounters often require a high degree of tolerance and warmth whilst under a multitude of assaults. We may experience kicks, scratches and screams, as we attempt to create participation so that we can provide rewards. Anger, punishment and retaliation offer no constructive pathway forward.

As mutuality and reciprocity strengthen, affectionate ties between persons grow which transcend time and place. Bonding becomes evident in the form of meaningful contact seeking and signalling behaviours. Most of us already have a core of friends, who can help us through the troubles and storms of life. The importance of friendship for community living to be successful is the theme of the King's Fund booklet, Ties and Connections (1988). 'It doesn't matter how bad we are, everyone needs friends. Friends are nice'.

Gentle teaching needs flexibility based on the nature and needs of particular persons rather than on our own. General prescriptions are of very limited help and techniques can be inherently dangerous. Peter Lomas (1987) sees 'the idealization of technique in human relations as the fundamental error'. In gentle teaching we use ourselves rather than simple techniques. Gentleness is a process of melting rather than breaking down defences, usually wisely erected. It requires tolerance, warmth and affection in encouraging behaviour which is meaningful, reciprocal and humanising.

The following extract from John McGee's book on gentle teaching (1987) shows how this transition can be made.

> Charles was a sixteen year old with mild mental handicap and aggressive behaviours, who spent considerable time in a 'time out box' at school. On beginning the gentle teaching programme, he was very disruptive and destructive. When asked to do something he would bite his arm, remove clothing, attempt to run out of the classroom and slap the teacher. Goals for Charles were to teach that human presence signalled safety, consistency and reward; that human interaction and participation predictably yielded reward; to defuse disruptive and destructive behaviours and create a bond with his teachers. An ignore - redirect - reward system was used to direct all interactions towards constructive responses. If Charles collapsed on the floor, the teaching materials and teacher worked at floor level. Interruption was used when

Charles tried to strike the teacher. The blow was blocked.

Ignoring and interrupting strategies were always passive and occurring simultaneously with redirection. Non-verbal redirection pointed to alternative possible responses instead of aggressive behaviour. Charles was provided with joyful and tactile praise for any participation even if disruptive behaviours were also happening. His day was structured with multiple opportunities to give reward, communicated by an affirmation of value, acceptance, approval, satisfaction and appreciation. Within a week Charles was no longer aggressive or destructive. He had learned that human participation yielded rewards.

A five year study of gentle teaching linked with the University of Nebraska (McGee, 1987) looked at outcomes for 73 handicapped persons with behavioural problems. The study examined the intensity of self injury before treatment divided into the three levels of high, medium and low; its intensity immediately before discharge; its intensity five years later. Over 86 per cent of referrals entered treatment with high intensity self-injurious behaviours. None displayed this level upon discharge or up to five years later. Remarkably, 72.6 per cent displayed no self injurious behaviour up to five years later.

Nearly two centuries ago, the modern history of mental handicap began with Itard's discovery of the Wild Boy of the Aveyron, Victor, living alone in the woods of southern central France. He seems to have been a young boy with mental handicaps, probably abandoned by relatives. Itard himself only once used aversive intervention (punishment) - a smack. It didn't seem to work and he regretted it for a long time afterwards.

Victor's relationship with Madame Guerin epitomised the desirable values and practice. She had a natural and easy going warmth, tolerance and affection. She loved Victor. His transformation into a sociable human being seemed to come much more from a natural bonding with her than from Itard's application of rigorous scientific method, although it is typical that a male oriented historical record celebrates the latter rather than the former.

Most paid staff working directly with people who have learning difficulties begin with a natural intimacy and solidarity with oppressed clients. They recognise the humanity and individuality of those they work with. Sadly, the professional courses and the acculturation of services knock that out of them. Senior people who no longer work directly with distressed people, deliver from on high their authoritative views on professionalised relationships. Often warm spontaneity is tainted by cold calculation. Love is replaced by ideologies. Staff learn a few crude techniques and long terms and unlearn the easy giving of self. They learn distance rather than closeness; objectivity rather than solidarity.

John O'Brien (1988) notes, 'mutual vulnerability increases as physical and social distance decrease, as weaker people gain control over resources, and as purposes and projects are shared. It grows from a decision to allow the other to become important to us, to touch us personally. To build mutual vulnerability, stay close to people who inflict pain on themselves and on others. Recognise that physical and social distance increases the likelihood of inflicting pain. Challenge everyday practices that build distance between staff and the people who rely on them'.

People with learning difficulties are among the most oppressed of all minorities. They are rejected and sentimentalised over as objects of pity, mawkishness and whimsy. There is a great danger that we may compound the overall oppression aimed at their submission. The system tries to break their spirit through enchaining both them and us. We need solidarity with them, recognising our mutual humanity. That means moving away from covert and dessicating technologies towards the freer giving of self. When we work towards their gradual and eventual liberation we automatically work towards our own.

References

Anderson, D.(1982) Social Work and Mental Handicap. Macmillan, (p. 33).

Bannister, D. (1983) The Internal Politics of Psychotherapy. In: Psychology and Psychotherapy'. Edited by David Pilgrim. Routledge and Kegan Paul.

Boadella, D. (1980). Violence in Therapy. Energy and Character, Journal of Bioenergetic Research, 2, No 1. Abbotsbury Publications.

King's Fund Centre..(1988). Ties and Connections - an Ordinary Community Life for People with Learning Difficulties (p.7).

Lally, J. (1988) When Anger is a Cry for Help. Community Living, 2,1.

Lomas, P. (1987) The Limits of Interpretation. Chapter Nine: The Misuse of Therapeutic Power.

McGee, J. et al. (1987)Gentle Teaching - a Non-Aversive Approach to Helping Persons with Mental Retardation. Human Sciences Press (p.21- 22 and 155-158).

O'Brien, J. (1988) Against Pain as a Tool in Professional Work on People with Severe Disabilities. Citizen Advocacy Association, Atlanta, Georgia, USA.

Rose, N. (1986) Psychiatry - the Discipline of Mental Health. In: (Editors: Miller, P. and Rose, N). The Power of Psychiatry. Polity Press.

Ross, A.O. (1981). Child Behaviour Therapy; Principles, Procedures and Behavioural Basis. Wiley (p.323 - 4).

Sharron, H. (1987) Changing Children's Minds - Feuerstein. Revolution in the Teaching of Intelligence. Souvenir Press.

Thomas, G. (1988). Journey into Madness - Medical Torture and the Mind Controllers. Bantam Press.

Yule, W. and **Carr, J.** (Editors) (1988). Behaviour Modification for People with Mental Handicaps (Second Edition). Croom Helm, (p.295).

Further reading

Berliner, Arthur K. (1986) Overcoming Obstacles to Counselling with the Mentally Retarded. British Journal of Mental Subnormality, 32, (1), January 1986.

Bernstein, Norman R. (1985) Psychotherapy of the Retarded Adolescent. University of Chicago.

Bicknell, J. (1983) The Psychopathology of Handicap. British Journal of Medical Psychology, 56, p.167-78.

Chidester, L. and **Menninger, K.** (1936) The Application of Psychoanalytic Methods to the Study of Mental Retardation. American Journal of Orthopsychiatry, 6, p. 616-25.

Clifford Scott, W. (1963) The Psychotherapy of the Mental Defective. Canadian Psychiatric Association Journal, 8, 5.

Frost, D. and **Taylor, K.** (1986). This is My Life. (Life Story Books), Community Care, 7 August 1986.

Gomersall, James D. (1984) Training and Supervision of Counsellors Working with People who are Mentally Handicapped. Mental Handicap, 12. September 1984.

Hodgson, C. (1987) Rewarding experience which helped clients make gains in self esteem. Social Work Today, 9 March 1987.

Hollins, S. and **Grimer, M.** (1988) Going Somewhere. Pastoral Care for People with Mental Handicap. SPCK.

Jukes, M. (1989) Self Determination - an Experiental Approach to Counselling for Mentally Handicapped People. Nursing Standard, 14 and 21 January, 1989.

Lee, W.Y. (1986) Human Sexuality: A Staff Training Manual for Individuals with Special Needs. Sexuality Clinic, Surrey Place Centre, 2 Surrey Place, Toronto, Canada M5S 2C2.

Lovett, H. (1985) Cognitive Counselling and Persons with Special Needs, Praeger.

Sarwer-Foner (1963) The Intensive Psychoanalytic Psychotherapy of a Brain-damaged Pseudo Mental Defective Fraternal Twin. Canadian Psychiatric Association Journal, Autumn.

Sinason, V. (1986) Secondary Mental Handicap and its Relationship to Trauma. Psychoanalytic Psychotherapy, 2, 2, p. 131-54.

Sinason, V. (1988) Richard III, Hephaestos and Echo: Sexuality and Mental/Multiple Handicap. Journal of Child Psychotherapy, 14, 2.

Stavrakaki,C. and **Klein, J.** (1986) Psychotherapies with the Mentally Retarded,

Psychiatric Perspectives on Mental Retardation Psychiatric Clinics of North America, 9, 4, December 1986.

St George's Hospital Medical School, Department of Psychiatry in Disability (1985). Video: The Last Taboo - exploration of bereavement counselling with people with learning difficulties.

Stokes, J. (1987) Insights from Psychotherapy. Paper presented at the International Symposium on Mental Handicap, Royal Society of Medicine, 25 February 1987.

Symington, N. (1981) The Psychotherapy of a Subnormal Patient. British Journal of Medical Psychology, 54, p.187-99.

Other publications by
GOOD IMPRESSIONS

PUTTING *PEOPLE* FIRST

A handbook on the practical application of
ordinary living principles.

By David and Althea Brandon.
Price £5.55 (including P&P).

'Lively, challenging, stimulating and readable - these are the appropriate
accolades for Putting PEOPLE First - an indispensable training manual.'
Social Work Today

FREE TO CHOOSE

An introduction to Service Brokerage.

By David Brandon and Noel Towe.
Price £5.70 (including P&P).

'Service brokerage is certain to receive great attention in the future and
this little book is the best available account at present. Read it and know
what it is to have your assumptions challenged.'
Nursing Times

Both available from Good Impressions Publishing Ltd,
Hexagon House, Surbiton Hill Road, Surbiton, Surrey KT6 4TZ.